Home Computers:
100 Icons that Defined a Digital Generation

Home Computers:
100 Icons that Defined a Digital Generation

Text by Alex Wiltshire
Photography by John Short

Produced in collaboration with The Centre for Computing History, Cambridge, UK

The MIT Press | Cambridge, Massachusetts | London, England

INTRODUCTION
THE COMPUTERS

CREDITS

Astrolabe; slide rule; difference engine. The computer has taken many forms over its long history. Antikythera mechanism; planimeter; arithmometer; Old Brass Brains. Each of these devices took in information, manipulated it according to a series of instructions, and then spat out results, helping to build structures, navigate space, reveal natural phenomena, and express concepts that would otherwise be beyond their creators' minds. They have quietly extended the limits of what humanity can do for centuries. But over a few short years at the end of the twentieth century, the computer experienced a revolution.

This was the moment in which the computer evolved from a tool designed to perform particular tasks for specialists into a general machine for all. It began taking part in everyday life, playing an essential role in homes and offices and changing the nature of work and leisure. It inspired generations of artists, engineers, and designers and helped form new fields of creativity, entertainment, and production. It made fortunes and took them, and it carved the essential foundation for an even wider digital revolution that was still to come.

During these tumultuous and defining years, the computer became electronic and digital, a humming, beige case that barged its way onto desks and trailed wires across rooms. It took over TV screens, presenting its users with the steady blink of an idle cursor and introducing them to arcane new languages that acted as an interface between them.

The microcomputer was another step along the computer's journey from clanking calculating mechanism to ubiquitous digital device, the result of a series of technological advances that brought about a crucial fusion of miniaturization and mass production. But it was also the child of many steps of theoretical development, which established ways of representing and transfiguring abstract numbers with minute pulses of electricity.

The key work was done in the first half of the twentieth century by mathematicians such as Alan Turing, Walther Bothe, Akira Nakashima, and Claude Shannon P. 24. They began to expand on older theories, such as that proposed by the seventeenth-century polymath Gottfried Wilhelm Leibniz, who, inspired by the I Ching, showed how binary numbers could perform logical and arithmetical functions. They went back to the papers of Charles Sanders Peirce, who had realized at the end of the nineteenth century that electrical circuits could perform logical functions. They explored ways in which logic gates could take binary inputs and produce outputs, and how data could be transported within the circuits of a machine.

The first culmination of their theory was realized by Max Newman and Tommy Flowers in 1943 as they completed Colossus, the first digital electronic computer, and in 1948 when the Manchester Baby became the first electronic computer that could store programs. But many more projects were developing across Europe and North America. Frequently built on the mechanical computers that directed weaponry and decoded communications during the Second World War, there was MIT's Whirlwind I, one of the first computers that could calculate in parallel, and ENIAC, the first general-purpose electronic computer, made for the US Army's Ballistic Research Laboratory.

It seems probable that once the machine thinking method had started, it would not take long to outstrip our feeble powers... They would be able to converse with each other

*to sharpen their wits. At some stage therefore, we should
have to expect the machines to take control.*
– Alan Turing

*I visualize a time when we will be to robots what dogs
are to humans. And I am rooting for the machines.*
– Claude Shannon

__ En masse, these machines inspired a wave of new invention
that further accelerated their development. In 1947, physicists
working at Bell Labs invented the transistor, a tiny semiconductor
that could control electronic signals. Replacing big, hot, and unreliable vacuum tubes, the transistor allowed electronics engineers to
build ever more intricate circuits, packing more components closer
together and raising their computational power.
__ By the 1960s, large companies such as IBM and Control
Data Corporation had grown to design and build mainframes.
Wardrobe-sized and stratospherically expensive, these large and
powerful computers were capable of storing and processing vast
sets of data such as population statistics and industrial outputs,
but they were confined to corporate headquarters and university
campuses. It would take another vital advance before the computer
could make the jump to the human scale of the garage workbench,
office desk, or the floor in front of the living-room TV.
__ That jump was called the silicon gate. In the late 1960s,
Federico Faggin at Fairchild Semiconductor in Palo Alto, California,
tried exchanging aluminium control gates in transistors for ones
made of polycrystalline silicon, and found they leaked less current,
required less space, and worked more reliably. Suddenly, the
multiple boards of components that comprised the innards of the
previous generations of computers could be compressed into tiny
integrated circuits. The microprocessor was born: a single chip that
could perform multiple functions at a far lower cost of production.
__ The microprocessor enabled mass production for the
mass market. The first to be commercially available was Intel's
4-bit 4004 in 1971. It held 2,300 transistors and its circuit lines
were 10 microns wide, and it was capable of performing 92,600
instructions per second. Two other microprocessors also appeared
around the same time: Garrett AiResearch's MP944, which was
first used as part of the Central Air Data Computer for F14 fighter
planes, and Texas Instruments' TMS 1000. None of them was
powerful – the 4004 could only really drive a calculator – and they
couldn't remotely compete in pure performance with mainframes.
But they were just the vanguard. Three years later, Intel shipped the
8-bit 8080, which was much quicker, supported a greater variety of
instructions, and could interface with other components more flex-
ibly, and it powered the very first generation of kit microcomputers.
__ Kits comprised circuit designs, build instructions, and
the components to make them, and they were the first computers
that made their way into family homes. Requiring soldering skills
and an understanding of electronics, not to mention a good deal
of money, kits such as the Altair 8800 `P. 22` were very much the
domain of hobbyists, enthusiasts who tinkered in their garages to
explore what a computer could do. The act of building them lent
insights into how they worked and gave opportunities to customize
and augment them with better parts.
__ That self-built nature naturally led to dreams of running
businesses: if you could make one for yourself, perhaps you could
make your own to sell? Especially in places such as Silicon Valley,

Fig. 1

Minivac 601 Manual: Designed to teach business employees how to
use computers, the Minivac 601 came with a comprehensive set of
manuals that featured friendly comic-book characters to help explain
the functions the computer could perform.

Fig. 2

Commodore VIC-20 packaging:
The box emphasized the simplicity
and form of the computer within.

Fig. 3

Packaging for Sord M5: The M5 was
expensive for a low-end computer of
its era, and its UK packaging helped
it to seem more desirable.

Fig. 4

Osborne 1 advertisement: The first portable computer
was highly appealing to business users, although its
advertising didn't quite give a sense of its full 11 kg
(24 lb) of weight.

where so much computer research and development was going on, a cottage industry of manufacturers who designed new kits and components grew. Magazines such as *Popular Electronics* rushed to support it, sharing circuit designs and program listings, reviewing products, and selling advertising.

___ Clubs started up, the most emblematic being the Homebrew Computer Club, which was founded by Gordon French and Fred Moore in Menlo Park, California, in March 1975. Their mission was to help make computers accessible to anyone, exchanging ideas and know-how over beers. They also published a newsletter that became the voice of Silicon Valley, with such material as a letter from Microsoft cofounder Bill Gates in February 1976 called 'An Open Letter to Hobbyists' that called out the scene for sharing his new company's software without paying for it:

> As the majority of hobbyists must be aware, most of you steal your software. Hardware must be paid for, but software is something to share. Who cares if the people who worked on it get paid?

> Is this fair? … The royalty paid to us, the manual, the tape and the overhead make it a break-even operation. One thing you do do is prevent good software from being written. Who can afford to do professional work for nothing? What hobbyist can put 3-man years into programming, finding all bugs, documenting his product and distribute for free? The fact is, no one besides us has invested a lot of money in hobby software. We have written 6800 BASIC, and are writing 8080 APL and 6800 APL, but there is very little incentive to make this software available to hobbyists. Most directly, the thing you do is theft.

___ The Homebrew Computer Club achieved its aim. Inspired by being one of the thirty-two people who attended its first meeting, Steve Wozniak designed and built the Apple I. While showing it off at a later meeting he met Steve Jobs, and together they founded the American company that arguably did the most to explore and expand the microcomputer's potential P.31.

___ Outside meetings, the newsletter helped to establish the language and shape of this new category of computers, establishing the concept of the '*personal computer*': a machine designed for a person's everyday individual use. After all, for most of the 1970s, there was no agreed form to the microcomputer. It wasn't until a more formalized commercial industry began to grow that it started to come in cases or be supplied with integrated keyboards, speakers, or displays. Computers weren't designed, in the sense that they were intended for a particular use. They were, more or less, just computers for computers' sake.

___ Until, that is, 1977. That year, three companies introduced new computers that were very much designed along the lines of discussions at the Homebrew Computer Club. Two out of the three – the Apple II and the PET 2001 – were specifically marketed as 'personal computers'; in other words, they were aimed at a new market of buyers who weren't looking to self-build or gain great insights into electronic circuitry. This new market, it was hoped, wanted off-the-shelf machines that came with every necessary component and only needed to be plugged into the wall before they worked.

___

In other words, it was time to popularize the microcomputer. As Jack Tramiel, CEO of Commodore, makers of the PET 2001 P.28, once put it:

> *Computers for the masses, not the classes.*

___ Commodore had spent years producing electronic calculators, giving the company an understanding of the popular end of the market, far from the rarified interests of computer hobbyists. Tramiel, a Holocaust survivor who had emigrated to the States from Poland, had built Commodore from nothing, first manufacturing typewriters and adding machines, then electronic calculators. Though he needed to be convinced by the idea of getting into computers, he went all-in once the market proved itself.

___ Tandy, maker of the TRS-80 P.27, was resolutely mainstream, a company that had started as a leather trader. It had Radio Shack, its own chain of electronics stores, and knew the market inside out. Still, its executives were wary of entering the nascent computer industry, but they quickly cashed in. The time was right, because the TRS-80's low price was right.

___ The price was right because the cost of components had fallen greatly over the late 1970s. After developing silicon gate technology and leaving Intel, where he had worked on the 4004 and 8080, Federico Faggin cofounded his own company, called Zilog, in 1974.

> *So, it was some time in December, it was on a Saturday, and I was debating what was the right thing to do. And that's when it hit me, it just hit me all at once. It was just like its own gestalt, and I said, 'Super-80!' And Super-80 … meant: a five-volt, depletion-load microprocessor with a lot of improvements which I already could see reasonably clearly, like twice as many registers, more instructions, more addressing modes, more bit-level instructions, a better interrupt structure yet, and designed as a family from the outset.*
> – Federico Faggin

___ Zilog's first microprocessor was the Z80, which was compatible with software written for the 8080 but ran far quicker, being made with 10,000 transistors compared to the 8080's 4,500. Together with the 6502, which was made by Commodore's chip-making subsidiary, MOS P.28, and just as cheap at just $25, the Z80 formed the backbone of many of the most important microcomputers of the late 1970s and 1980s. But the differences between these two chips drew up battle lines between the computers that used them. Software written for the instruction sets and architecture of a Z80-powered TRS-80 would need to be rewritten entirely to work for a 6502-powered Apple II.

___ Even computers running on the same microprocessor weren't compatible with each other, due to differences between the software and languages that ran on them, as well as the specifics of the way their memory, ROMs, and other components were wired together. In the goldrush that began with the launch of the first home computers, computer manufacturers were more interested in getting their machines to market than forming standards. Competition was everything.

___ The sheer number of new computers and new models of existing computers that appeared across Europe and North America in the early 1980s is staggering. They spread so fast that it was

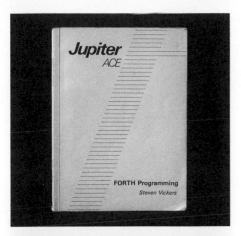

Fig. 5

Fig. 6

Fig. 7

Fig. 8

Jupiter Ace Forth programming guide: Written by its software designer to document its unconventional use of Forth rather than BASIC, the Ace's programming guide is still in print today.

TRS-80 Color Computer Operation Manual: Introduces the CoCo as 'an exciting tool for an infinite variety of uses – home finances, education, recreation, amusement and amazement'.

Sinclair QL packaging: Sinclair's simplicity of presentation, which emphasizes the product, prefigured Apple's minimalist packaging design.

Commodore PET User Manual: The PET's manual was surprisingly austere for that of a computer designed for the home, but it did encourage owners to contact Commodore with questions, giving it more of a human touch.

hard to keep count, or understand how many were being sold, but the United States Census Bureau estimated that by October 1984, 8.2 per cent of American households owned a computer, and that just over 70 per cent of those households had bought their computer after 1982. By 1993, 22.8 per cent of households had one.

— The greatest proliferation of new computer launches was perhaps in Western Europe, where multitudes of new companies popped up across its patchwork of different countries, particularly in the UK. There, the revolution was kicked off almost entirely by one person: Clive Sinclair. Sinclair encouraged an inventive approach to designing computers, all in aid of making products that were extraordinarily small and cheap, and featured industrial design that made them look like they had come from the future. To fuel this vision, he founded a series of companies in Cambridge, such as Science of Cambridge and Sinclair Research. Many of the staff he hired would go on to found their own companies, such as Acorn Computers and Jupiter Cantab.

— The British computing magazines that sprang up to report on the constant flow of product announcements and rumours that streamed out of the local industry called Sinclair 'Uncle Clive', portraying him as a loveable eccentric who brought them such fabulous presents as the ZX Spectrum. But he was also an astute businessman, unafraid to take risks if it meant releasing at the right time and at the right price. The ZX80 was profoundly underpowered by the standards of the American machines coming out at the time, but he could market it as costing under £100. A year later, the ZX81 barely improved on the ZX80 other than to cut nearly a third off its already low price P. 71.

— The household, as Tramiel and Sinclair had realized, was extremely price-conscious, and as competition rose during the early 1980s a war raged that nearly sank the entire industry. It started as Commodore and Texas Instruments jostled to make their VIC-20 and TI-99/4A more appealing, but it was galvanized by Sinclair, who had teamed up with Timex to release a version of the ZX81 in the US called the Timex Sinclair 1000 P. 124. It cost under $100 and quickly won over a quarter of the market, forcing other manufacturers to further drop their prices. Texas Instruments lost so much money that it gave up on computers entirely. Atari was sold by its parent company, Warner. Even Timex Sinclair, less than a year and a half after it entered, got out of the US market, calling it 'volatile'.

> People think computers will keep them from making mistakes. They're wrong. With computers you make mistakes faster.
> – Adam Osborne

— The UK market was just as turbulent, experiencing a crash at the end of 1984. Manufacturers had underestimated demand for computers in the run-up to Christmas 1983 and undersupplied retailers, so for Christmas 1984 they shipped thousands to ensure they wouldn't run out. But demand had dropped and the retailers, which commanded sale-or-return terms, dumped unsold stock back on their makers. Prices collapsed, and so did many firms.

— By the end of the 1980s, no matter how large or small, few of the companies that founded the home computer revolution still made them. Osborne, Dragon Data, Spectravideo, and Oric all burned bright and disappeared. Sinclair Research was subsumed into Amstrad, which itself was about to shift its attention away from home computers. Tandy gave up on them entirely.

⎯　Another key challenge was the speed at which technology was developing. Between the release of the first personal computers in 1977 and 1985, they jumped through an entire generation of microprocessors, from 8-bit to 16-bit, and from keyboard-driven command-line interfaces to mouse-driven graphical ones. Every new model had to thread the needle of being powerful enough to be appealing, cheap enough to build, and reliable enough to minimize returns. As they featured more memory and faster clock speeds, and supported more peripherals, fit became more complicated to fulfil each need.

⎯　One particularly rife engineering problem was that of electromagnetic interference. Integrated circuits naturally create electromagnetic emissions, but when they are connected to other components, such as wires and heatsinks, these emissions tend to radiate more widely and encroach on TV and radio signals. Many computers, such as the Apple III P. 60 and TRS-80 Model I P. 27, ended up being discontinued as a result of emissions that broke US government regulations.

⎯　Some computers attempted to sidestep the issue, such as the Apple II, which didn't feature a TV output because the RF modulator required by a TV connector would spew out more electromagnetic interference. More commonly, they would use metal shields to ensure the interference sat within accepted levels – the Atari 800 had all its circuitry encased in a 2mm thick box – but these shields raised manufacturing prices and could cause the machines to overheat. One example is the shield that Commodore hurriedly added to the 128, which doubled as a heatsink. Bad contacts between the shield and chips tended to make it overheat and malfunction; the most common solution was to simply remove the shield.

⎯　But still new computers were being released. For all the excitement and noise around them, there were those who believed the lack of standardization was holding the industry back. They wondered about how they might set an agreed format that many manufacturers could follow so that software was cross-compatible. One such person was Kazuhiko Nishi, a college dropout, computer enthusiast, and writer who had founded a magazine and game publisher in Japan called ASCII. He took a quiet role in a great number of important developments in the early history of home computers, gaining reputation and influence that allowed him to bring together Japan's most notable manufacturers in supporting a format called MSX P. 133.

I started the company by publishing magazines. Because I didn't have any money when we started, this was the only thing I could do. Also, no computers existed on the market. So I wrote articles about what kind of computer would come. It was really a type of propaganda. Then we published books, namely translations of American technology books. Then we published software – a lot of software. We became an agent of Microsoft and imported Microsoft software. Then I discovered what set the boundaries for software. The ceiling is set by semiconductors. So if you can do something creative with semiconductors, we can make the best use of them by combining them with the right software.
– Kazuhiko Nishi

Fig. 9

Sinclair ZX Spectrum packaging: Adding value, usually with packed-in software, was vital at the low end of the British market in the mid-1980s.

Fig. 10

Dragon disk drive unit advertisement: Priced at £275 on its release, the Dragon 32's disk drive add-on cost a great deal more than the Dragon 32 itself.

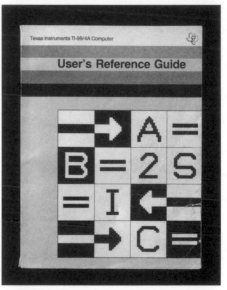

Fig. 11

TI-99/4A *User's Reference Guide*: Given that one of the TI-99/4A's advantages over the previous TI-99 was its ability to display lower-case characters, it seems curious that its manual's cover didn't showcase them.

Fig. 12

Atari 400 BASIC manual: Its writer, Bob Albrecht, was an important figure in the early computer scene, a regular at the Homebrew Computer Club, and a founder of the *Dr Dobbs* newsletter.

MSX was a specification of off-the-shelf parts that was cleverly assembled to make the most of them, and it became a major format in Japan, parts of Europe and many other countries dotted around the world. But although it evolved through several generations, it made little impact in the two markets that did the most to determine the future of computing – the US and the UK – and it withered in the face of the more organic trends towards standardization that were to come.

___ Despite the lack of hardware standards, some software standards did start to coalesce. The first generations of hobbyists formed software companies that would go on to help define the ongoing evolution of the computer, such as Microsoft, which would provide the means of working with a computer by writing versions of the BASIC programming language for many different systems.

___ BASIC became the de facto language and operating environment of the early home computer, partly because it was small and thus able to fit into tiny (and cheap) ROMs. But each computer featured a different variant of BASIC, with new commands and tweaks to support its particular idiosyncrasies. Knowing Sinclair BASIC didn't mean you woud immediately know how to boot up a game on a Commodore 64 P.79.

___ Games, too, needed to be ported to each system. Game publishers employed not only game designers but also programmers who knew how to convert a game written for one system to another. Each computer had certain ways of writing its graphics to the TV screen, different colour palettes, different sound capabilities, different amounts of memory. These technical peculiarities gave games made for a particular machine a distinctive signature. Colour graphics flickering with attribute clash would be recognizably be the product of a Sinclair ZX Spectrum P. 91, while richly arpeggiated, multi-channel music had to have come from a Commodore 64. These signatures became stylistic banners for their fans, and negotiating their strengths and weaknesses well became badges of skill for game creators.

___ Naturally, games were system-sellers. Families would buy computers with their children in mind, often with the idea that the computer would somehow educate them, while children wanted the system with the best games. Some manufacturers understood this better than others: for the VIC-20, Commodore specifically commissioned ports of games by text adventure writer Scott Adams, and they greatly contributed to its initial appeal P. 56.

___ Good game designers were therefore in hot demand. Many of them were initially merely computer enthusiasts who taught themselves to code at the BASIC prompt. The way computers required users to learn commands to do the simplest task, such as loading a game, subtly instructed them in the basics of programming, and they were further supported by magazines that published long BASIC program listings, which, if they managed to avoid making mistakes, would result in functioning games. If they *did* make a mistake, then debugging their code would help them understand what went wrong and hint at ways they could tweak it to make the game behave differently. And since games copied from listings were invariably terrible, there was every encouragement to make better ones.

The beauty was that all that you needed to learn to program was in the box. So there was an excellent book … that told you how to program. It took you through the steps with a fairly steep learning curve, but beautifully

laid out. I think that was very, very helpful, to the extent that by halfway through the book it was teaching you how to program an assembler. It didn't hang around, but that was great. It meant that I and a lot of other people in the same generation could be self-directed, we could learn on our own.
– David Braben

___ Game publishers advertised in those same magazines, asking for readers to submit their games for review and potential publishing in return for outrageously low fees. It was an exploitative system, and it existed in every country where the home computer took hold, whether the UK, France, Japan, or Czechoslovakia. But a few of these young game makers became famous, and some rich, from John Romero, co-creator of *Doom*, to Jeff Minter, best known for his action games for Commodore machines, and David Braben, who co-wrote the staggeringly ambitious *Elite* for the BBC.

___ BASIC wasn't the only operating environment that early computers used. Business machines tended to favour Digital Research's CP/M, for which many of the big office applications, such as Wordstar, were written. CP/M gained that position partly because it made it somewhat easier to convert applications for CP/M between different computers. This property encouraged software makers to support CP/M, and the number of applications available made it attractive to users. It was a virtuous cycle.

___ Sometimes, however, a single piece of brilliance could drive the popularity of a system. When VisiCorp wrote VisiCalc for the Apple II in 1979, this proto-spreadsheet quickly became the computer's first 'killer app'. Not that Apple was looking for business applications. Jobs had intended the Apple II for the home: simple, easy to use, and ready to bring the wonders of computers to families. But because of VisiCalc, which introduced an entirely new way of viewing and calculating with numbers in tables, the Apple II sold best among businesses.

___ Then Microsoft's DOS came along, which IBM had chosen to be the operating system for its entry into the world of microcomputers, the 5150 P. 66. IBM hadn't meant to found a universal standard for computers, but the PC, as the 5150 became known, would go on to take over both the world of business and home computing. It steadily suffocated every other format with its flexibility, support of multifarious peripheral devices, and the ability to evolve with new generations of technology while maintaining compatibility with older ones.

Every breakthrough business idea begins with solving a common problem. The bigger the problem, the bigger the opportunity. I discovered a big one when I took apart an IBM PC. I made two interesting discoveries: The components were all manufactured by other companies, and the system that retailed for $3,000 cost about $600 in parts.
– Michael Dell

___ In building the 5150 out of standardized parts, rather than the custom chips that other formats tended to use to reduce costs, IBM unwittingly allowed others to copy its design. First Columbia Data Products, then Compaq and a flurry of new upstarts, were able to piggyback on IBM's vast marketing campaign, which did the work of establishing the PC among businesses and attracting the software it needed to be successful. All but one of the

Fig. 13

Commodore 64 packaging: A rainbow heralded the 64's new graphics abilities; each of the box's nine hues matched one in the 64's palette of sixteen colours.

Fig. 14

Apple iMac discs: Apple packed in its own software with its new computers, keenly positioning them in the new realm of multimedia creation.

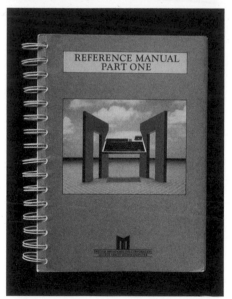

Fig. 15

Acorn BBC Master *Reference Manual:* Like all the user guides for the BBC series of computers, the Master's manual was ring-bound and written in plain language, making it a perfect computer-side reference.

Fig. 16

BASIC manual for ZX80: While the operating manuals of its successors, the ZX81 and Spectrum, featured science-fiction-inflected artwork and graphic design, the ZX80's manual played it simple.

manufacturers that did survive into the 1990s – even Atari and Commodore – stopped making their own designs and began to build PCs alongside nimble new companies such as Dell and Gateway, which embraced a new world of consumer-driven customized options and direct selling.

___ The custodian of this new format was not IBM but Microsoft. First with DOS and then with Windows, Microsoft provided the PC with a software foundation on which all its sound cards, spreadsheets, and a growing range of games could run. The computer steadily became less defined by its individual specifications and more by the software that ran on it. And that helped it take an ever-widening role in homes as a place to do homework, catalogue CD collections, browse the Internet, do the accounts, or write letters.

___ That shift really started accelerating once the GUI (graphical user interface) gained ascendancy. The first to come to market was made by Apple for the Lisa P.146 and released in 1983, closely followed by CP/M maker Digital Research's GSX, while Microsoft was already working on its own, first called Interface Manager and later renamed as Windows for its release in 1985. But all these operating systems were based on research into computer interfaces done during the 1970s at Xerox PARC. That single source means that we take representations of data as 'files' and the screen as a 'desktop' so much for granted today that it's hard to know what it would be to use a computer if Xerox's scientists and designers had come to different conclusions.

___ The moment the GUI would snap into focus, however, was in 1984 when Apple launched the Macintosh, which was designed primarily to make the computer more accessible. As Steve Jobs, who eagerly led the project as an exemplar of what he felt a computer should be, said:

> Most people have no concept of how an automatic transmission works, yet they know how to drive a car. You don't have to study physics to understand the laws of motion to drive a car. You don't have to understand any of this stuff to use Macintosh.

___ It was this idea that propelled the computer through its next revolution, which was when manufacturers unmoored the computer from the tabletop. Portable – or 'luggable' – computers had been around since the early 1980s, packing tiny CRT monitors into their large and heavy cases, and usually needing to be plugged into a power source to run. It wasn't until LCD technology made flat-screens possible that computers could become truly portable: small enough to fit into the lap and battery-powered so they could be used anywhere. A schism developed between these early laptops and even smaller portable computers, which gradually settled into new typologies – palmtops and PDAs.

___ And all the while, computers began to settle more naturally into the home. Most early machines were resolutely functional, their design usually at the mercy of their budgets and specifications. It couldn't be easy to design a beautiful object with an integrated tape player and thick electromagnetic shielding that was cheap to build. When their designers did care about appearance, computers tended to look towards the likes of *2001: A Space Odyssey*, hoping its futurism would lend them a sense of technological promise.

___ Rick Dickinson, industrial designer of the ZX80 and Spectrum, went a long way to finding a new design language for computers that managed to make them neatly characterful and desirable. But it wasn't until the Macintosh that they began to more seriously combine a distinct character with practical usability and drive the same aesthetic values into the software that ran on them. The Macintosh was a holistically designed object, from silicon to screen, with an operating system that looked and behaved like it fitted with its exterior.

___ Still, computers' headlong rush into the new meant that these ideas were a luxury. PCs remained encased in beige boxes, a form that even Apple went back to for some of its darker years in the late 1980s and early 1990s. But home computers nevertheless kept becoming more essential to everyday life, emerging from bedrooms and offices and becoming centres of family activity. As processor speeds increased, and memory and storage grew, they became more visual and rich with sound and movement. They became more responsive and dynamic, native to the same ways of seeing and representing the world as us. Home computers had become more human. They had become for everyone.

A complete implementation of the
FORTH language for the ATOM

ACORNSOFT
FORTH

SYNTH
PICNIC
TOCCATA
SEASIDE

ACORNSOFT
SYNTHESISER

ATARI®
HOME
COMPUTER

ATARI

USER'S GUIDE

INTERNATIONAL

ns Company

STARGATE
GOMOKU
ROBOTS

ACORNSOFT
GAMES PACK
8

ASTEROI
SUB-HUN
BREAKO

ACORNSOFT
GAMES PA

CASIO **MSX** PERSONAL COMPUTER
カシオMSXパーソナルコンピュータMX-10

MX-10

CASIO

MIDIで音楽も楽しめる

パソコンが簡単に使える

オリジナルゲームをつくる

計算・データ処理にも使え

ワープロにも使え

Atari *User's Guide*   Acorn Atom software

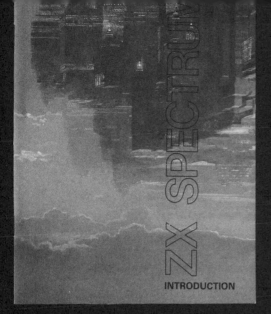

The manuals produced for early home computers were often styled to emphasize a sense of clean and efficient modernity. Using lots of Helvetica and simple imagery, they contrived a sense of calm technical authority for owners who were likely new to using a computer. One of the few companies that dreamed a little wider about the place its computers should take in its users' lives was Sinclair, which revelled in its products' industrial design, establishing a marketing philosophy that even Apple hadn't yet considered.

Sinclair ZX81 packaging

Cambridge Z88 packaging

Apple III Owner's Guide

THE COMPUTERS

MANUFACTURER
Scientific Development Corporation

AVAILABLE
1961

TECHNICAL DATA
6 bits memory

ORIGIN
United States

Claude Shannon invented many things. He designed the toy that, when you flip a switch on its top, opens a door and reaches out an arm to flip the switch back and close the door again. He created a flame-throwing trumpet, a machine that could solve Rubik's Cubes, and Theseus, a 'mouse' moved by electromagnets that could learn its way through a maze.

He also helped shape what became the computer. In 1937, at the age of 22, he wrote a Master's thesis in which he demonstrated performing arithmetical calculation using the on/off positions of switches in electronic circuits, and in doing so helped form the foundational concept of how computers work. And in 1948 he invented information theory, a new way of thinking about how data could be communicated.

Though it wasn't as foundational, in many ways, the Minivac 601 is the culmination of his work. With this kit computer, he intended to teach business people about how digital computers worked, introducing them to assembler language and binary arithmetic at the dawn of the computer age. Its electromechanical relays worked as both logic switches and storage, six switches provided binary inputs, and a motorized dial that acted as an input for decimal and hexadecimal numbers also worked as a display alongside six indicator lights. Its beautifully presented manuals provided a series of tutorials and, most importantly, explained how a number of games, including tic-tac-toe, could be played on it.

At $85, the Minivac 601 quickly interested hobbyists and educationalists, but its maker, SDC (Scientific Development Corporation), found that businesses weren't so keen to buy it as a training tool to prepare their employees for a new way of working. The solution? SDC exchanged the Minivac 601's sky-blue case for gunmetal grey, tweaked some of the switches, added more patch cords for connecting its components, and began selling the new Minivac 6010 the following year for $479. Now not so toy-like, it sold in its hundreds.

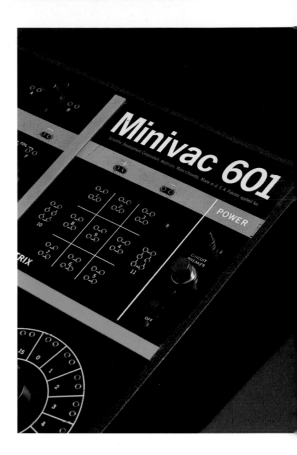

SDC MINIVAC 601

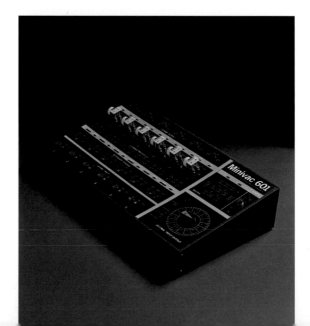

MITS
ALTAIR 8800B

ORIGIN
United States

TECHNICAL DATA
Intel 8080 at 2 MHz, 1024 B RAM

AVAILABLE
January 1975

MANUFACTURER
Micro Instrumentation and
Telemetry Systems

The computer on the front cover of *Popular Electronics* that jumpstarted the home computer revolution was a fake. Published in January 1975, the cover featured an empty metal box with rows of LEDs and switches on its fascia. Due to a courier strike, the only prototype yet made had been lost somewhere between its maker's headquarters in Albuquerque and the magazine's New York office, but the computer, the Altair 8800, was real: the product of a bold gamble that its creator, Ed Roberts, hoped would save his company.

Roberts had cofounded MITS (Micro Instrumentation and Telemetry Systms) in 1969 to design electronics kits for model rocket enthusiasts, but his real interest was in computers and in 1970 he designed the MITS 816, a pocket calculator that could add, subtract, divide and multiply. MITS received hundreds of orders per month and began to expand, but two years later, larger companies were marketing calculators at prices below MITS's cost of materials. Facing debt, MITS laid off staff and Roberts looked to the home kit computer for rescue.

'World's First Minicomputer Kit to Rival Commercial Models … SAVE OVER $1,000,' read the *Popular Electronics* cover. Until the Altair 8800, computers were large and expensive and confined to universities and corporations. But Roberts figured that Intel's newly launched 8080 microprocessor would power a full computer. To bring down the chip's cost down he made an agreement with Intel to buy 1,000, raising a loan to fund

them. MITS's fortunes hung in the balance, but the *Popular Electronics* cover worked. At $439 for the kit and $621 for a pre-assembled computer the company couldn't keep up with orders, and by August 1975 they had sold 5,000.

Two students named Bill Gates and Paul Allen also noticed the cover and approached Roberts to ask if he would buy their BASIC programming language. Roberts agreed to see a demo, but they hadn't yet written it; they didn't even have an Altair to develop it on. Gates and Allen scrambled to make an Intel 8080 emulator on Harvard's PDP-10, and Allen only finished writing the last bits of their Altair BASIC demo on the plane to Albuquerque. Another gamble paid off: Roberts liked it enough to commission it. Altair BASIC became Microsoft's first-ever product.

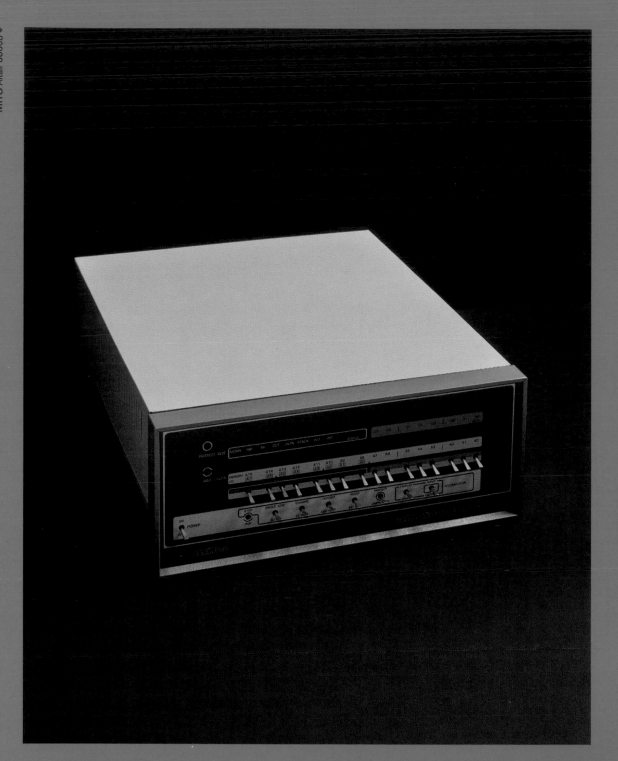

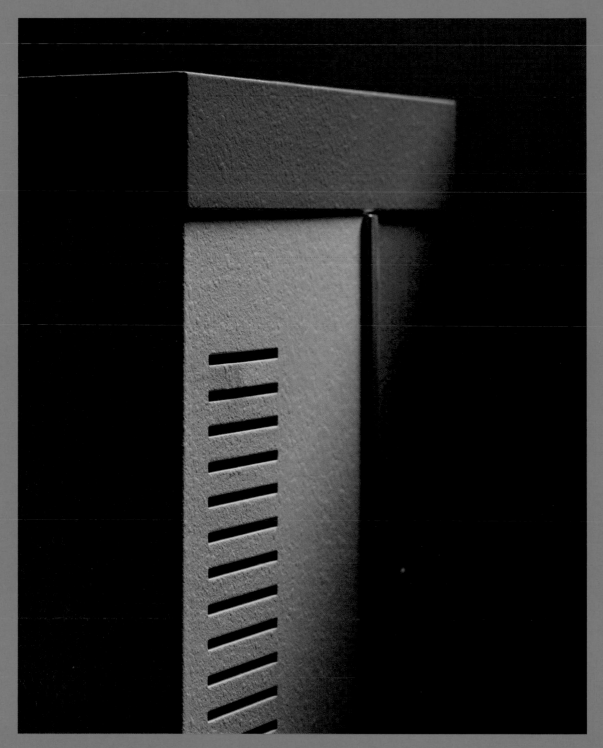

MANUFACTURER
Tandy Corporation

AVAILABLE
July 1980

TECHNICAL DATA
Zilog Z80 at 2 MHz, 4 KB RAM

ORIGIN
United States

RADIO SHACK TRS-80 MODEL III

In 1977, three computers were launched that sparked a revolution: the Commodore PET **P.29**, the Apple II **P.31** and the TRS-80 Model I. Each could be taken out of its box and switched on with no assembly required, and each was available at a low price on every high street.

As owner of a US-wide retail chain, Tandy had a natural eye for the popular market. Its executives, then, had been highly sceptical when a product buyer called Don French tried to convince them to start producing computer kits, which were beginning to sell in their thousands. Eventually, he managed to talk them into visiting National Semiconductor to watch how it was incorporating its SC/MP microprocessor into kit computers. There they met a young engineer called Steve Leininger, and they asked him to design a kit computer that Tandy could sell for less than $200.

Tandy's leadership still wasn't convinced. When a customer returned a digital clock kit as faulty, Leininger discovered they had misunderstood the assembly instructions and soldered every component to the bottom of its board. Hearing about it, the head of buying tried to block the project: how could Tandy's customers follow a computer kit's much more complex instructions? Leininger responded by ditching the kit idea. Instead, Tandy would sell an entirely preassembled computer.

CEO Charles Tandy didn't know about the project until February 1977, when Leininger was ready to show him the final product, a wedge of silver-grey plastic that shipped with a display and a tape player. His initial response was hardly positive: 'Who wants a computer?' But he nevertheless approved a first production run of 1,000, which the team upped to 3,500 in order to gain a discount for ordering a higher volume. It happened that 3,500 was *also* how many Radio Shack stores Tandy owned. The team figured that if a store could not sell its machine, that store could use it in its own office. But the TRS-80 was a success, greatly supported by Tandy's nation-spanning retail and marketing machine and a $400 price tag. Various updated models followed, including, in July 1980, the Model III, which was fully integrated and featured a better keyboard and space for two disk drives. Over the next decade, Tandy, which was founded as a leather trader, would become the biggest computer manufacturer in the world.

Radio Shack TRS-80 Model III, disk drives ↑

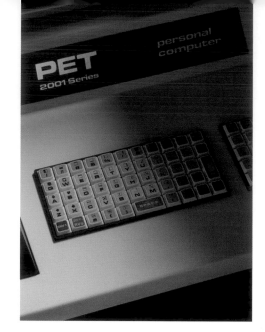

ORIGIN
United States

TECHNICAL DATA
MOS 6502 at 1 MHz, 4 KB–8 KB RAM

AVAILABLE
October 1977

MANUFACTURER
Commodore International

Commodore's entrance into the computer market was the result of a disaster. Then again, the company had already ridden many waves of opportunity and potential calamity. Its history began when Jack Tramiel, a Polish Auschwitz survivor, emigrated to the US. He found work driving cabs, running a typewriter repair shop on the side, and he founded Commodore Business Machines in 1955 when he won a contract to produce a Czechoslovakian typewriter company's designs. He steadily grew his company, but in the late 1950s many North American firms went out of business as Japan started to export typewriters. Tramiel, however, looked to a new opportunity: mechanical adding machines. Business recovered, and Commodore went public on the New York Stock Exchange. Then, in the late 1960s, Commodore's market changed again as Japan started to export its own adding machines. Again Tramiel pivoted and survived, exchanging mechanical calculators for electronic ones.

Then the calculator business failed. One of the main suppliers of integrated circuits for calculators in the early 1970s was Texas Instruments, and in 1975 it decided to drastically raise its prices. Many manufacturers were forced out of business, in turn endangering chip maker MOS Technology. Although MOS had just launched the 6502 microprocessor, most of its revenue came from supplying a calculator market that was now in tumult. Tramiel knew that if MOS fell, it would take its supply of integrated circuits with it, so Commodore bought MOS in 1976, instantly gaining a chip-design and manufacturing subsidiary of its very own. One particularly valuable asset was 6502 designer Chuck Peddle, who convinced Tramiel to get into computers.

Tramiel had always understood the mass market, so Commodore's first computer, the PET 2001, was designed for it. It cost $795 and came with an integrated screen, tape recorder, and keyboard – everything a new computer owner needed, right out of the box – and it appealed widely across both home users and businesses. The PET founded a long-running and best-selling series of computers and represented a new direction for Commodore P.56. Its awkward 'chiclet' keyboard, though? No one liked that.

COMMODORE PET 2001

MANUFACTURER
Apple Computer

AVAILABLE
January 1983

TECHNICAL DATA
Synertek 6502 at 1 MHz, 64 KB RAM

ORIGIN
United States

APPLE IIE

Not every groundbreaking computer was about delivering blistering power and speed. On its release in June 1977, the Apple II featured the same processor, running at the same clock speed, as the Apple I, the single-board kit that computer engineer Steve Wozniak had designed the previous year. But it launched what would become the most valuable company in the world and changed attitudes about how computers should look, run, and feel. Rather than power, the Apple II was about refinement.

Steve Wozniak began to design the Apple II's insides while still a Hewlett-Packard employee, but he soon left to join Apple full-time, working to a philosophy that he set out in *Byte* magazine as follows: 'A personal computer should be small, reliable, convenient to use and inexpensive.' In order to make the machine as economic as possible, he used ingenious ways of controlling the frequencies of each component and avoiding interruptions of the video stream without requiring extra chips and circuits. Although the base 4-KB model cost a hefty $1,298, it could display colour, unlike the other all-in-one computers that came out that year.

Apple's founder, Steve Jobs, recruited Jerry Manock, a freelance industrial designer, to create the Apple II's casing for $1,500, asking for a machine that would sell beyond the hobbyist community. Jobs didn't want fans or vents; he knew that a major source of heat was the power supply, so he asked engineer Rod Holt to design one that oscillated on and off far quicker than standard ones. Jobs claimed its design was as important as Wozniak's celebrated logic board.

Various versions followed the Apple II's release, including the Apple II Plus in 1979, which had improved graphics and included Apple BASIC in its ROM, and the IIe in 1983. The 'e' stood for 'enhanced'; aside from more RAM, it also had a full ASCII character set, which included lower-case letters and the logo-adorned modifier key that can still be found on Apple keyboards today. Remaining in production all the way up to November 1993, the IIe was the most popular model of this legendary computer, but many more were to come P. 60.

CAUTION: UNDER NO CIRCUMSTANCES IS THIS CASE TO BE OPENED. THIS POWER SUPPLY IS NOT USER-SERVICEABLE AND THERE ARE DANGEROUS HIGH VOLTAGES INSIDE THE POWER SUPPLY CASE. IN THE EVENT OF DIFFICULTY, NOTIFY APPLE COMPUTER LTD.; OR YOUR DEALER FOR PROMPT SERVICE.

POWER SUPPLY SERIAL # A2M0030- № 568793

apple computer ltd

ORIGIN
United States

TECHNICAL DATA
Rockwell 6502 at 1 MHz, 1 KB RAM

AVAILABLE
1978

MANUFACTURER
Rockwell

At just $25, MOS Technology's 6502 was the cheapest microprocessor available when it launched in 1975. Along with its descendents, it would come to serve as the core of many of the machines that drove the home computer revolution, from the Apple II P.31 to the Commodore 64 P.79. In fact, it's still used today. But that success only came after a long struggle to get computer makers to try it out, from corporations who thought its low price was a scam to hobbyists who weren't used to microprocessor manufacturers taking an interest in them.

Unlike other chip manufacturers, MOS welcomed enquiries from any potential customer and encouraged everyone to copy its technical literature – all to help broadcast the 6502's good qualities. MOS also tried to expand awareness by releasing, in 1976, a single-board machine called the KIM-1, which, when connected to a terminal and disk drive, was a fully functional computer. Cheap at only $245, the KIM-1 was a success among both hobbyists and professionals. It made enough waves to attract the attention of manufacturing conglomerate Rockwell, which decided to second-source the 6502, buying the licence from MOS so it could build the microprocessor itself. Rockwell designed an expanded version of the KIM-1 called the AIM-65.

So that it could launch at $375, the AIM-65 was bare-bones, but it featured a built-in keyboard and a 20-character LED display, and its 20-character thermal printer could be set to print out every line that appeared on the display. Supported by a ROM that came with software that listed and edited memory registers, executed programs, and assembled and disassembled code, it was an ideal development computer, especially for programmers learning the 6502's functions (and how to work around what it couldn't do). The AIM-65's developer tools cost far less than their established counterparts, making it a valuable tinkerer's machine: it ended up being used to control the hydraulics on floats in the Pasadena Tournament of Roses, and it ran digital audio pioneer MTU's early real-time music synthesizer.

ROCKWELL AIM-65

MANUFACTURER
Intertec Data Systems

AVAILABLE
September 1979

TECHNICAL DATA
Zilog Z80A at 4 MHz, 16 KB RAM

ORIGIN
United States

If you were asked to imagine the most bombastically named and futuristically designed 1970s computer, you would be hard-pressed to come up with a better example than the Superbrain. With a curvilinear all-in-one injection-moulded casing, which featured a soft-touch coating, it exuded the utopian promise of a technological future. Of the machines of its age, the Superbrain had a particular focus on design and user experience, which perhaps came as a result of the fact that Intertec was founded by former IBM employee William Wells as a one-man-band maker of terminals. Terminals, after all, were all about being an interface between user and computer.

Inside the swell of the Superbrain's shell were two Z80 microprocessors, one of which was used to control its dual 170-KB disk drives. It ran the CP/M operating system. CP/M was first written in 1974 by computer scientist Gary Kildall, who founded a company called Intergalactic Digital Research to license out his creation, but soon rather sensibly removed the first word, making it simply Digital Research. CP/M became a staple operating system among early microcomputers because the way it was written made it easily adaptable for new systems as they arrived on the market. Digital Research and Microsoft would stand together as the software companies that guided the computer through the 1980s, though Microsoft's DOS would come to rule the microcomputer after Kildall decided not to take IBM's deal to licence CP/M for its forthcoming PC P. 66.

Despite its flashy looks, the Superbrain found most use in offices, where its twin floppy drives could store and manage reams of business data. Along with hard-disk upgrades and new versions that featured higher-density floppy-disk drives and network support, it helped Intertec post $17 million in revenue in 1981. But the company's fortunes started to turn in 1983 when IBM's PC began to reshape the office computer market, its rectilinear beige box taking a sad precedence over Intertec's futurism.

INTERTEC SUPERBRAIN

ORIGIN
United States

TECHNICAL DATA
Zilog Z80 at 2.1 MHz, 4 KB RAM

AVAILABLE
April 1978

MANUFACTURER
Exidy

EXIDY
SORCERER

When Paul Terrell opened The Byte Shop in Menlo Park, California, in December 1975, he founded one of the first game retailers in the world. The hobby scene was kicking off, but Terrell had a more expansive view of what computers should be. He wanted to sell fully assembled machines that came with every necessary accessory, so that they would appeal to a wider market than simply hobbyists. When he became the first stockist of the single-board Apple I, Terrell sold it with a monitor and keyboard, and he helped convince Jobs and Wozniak that their next computer would be an all-in-one.

The idea stuck with Terrell in November 1977, when he jumped out of the business he had helped to found. The Apple II P. 31, PET P. 28, and TRS-80 P. 27 were proving he was right, and computer retail was hard, with manufacturers holding a lot of control over what pricing and stock the shops could negotiate. So, while the going was good, he sold up and went to talk to two friends about building a home computer that balanced Apple II-level graphics with PET's ease of use. Those friends were Pete Kauffman and Howell Ivy, founders of coin-op game maker Exidy, which had pioneered the high-score table. Terrell had been impressed by the graphics capabilities of games such as *Death Race*, which was controversially centred around running over human-like figures, and felt they would be perfect to build his computer. Exidy agreed.

Terrell named the computer Sorcerer ('Computers are like magic to people,' he said), and features such as the ROM PAC might have seemed just like magic. This cartridge slot, similar to the one found on the Atari 2600, allowed users to plug in new programs (and games) without having to load from tape or disk, and Exidy packed in Microsoft BASIC, a word processor, and an assembler for programmers. But despite strong orders in 1978, Exidy failed to market the $895 Sorcerer widely enough in the US. It sold well in the Netherlands and Australia, but Exidy pulled the plug on it in 1981.

ORIGIN
United States

TECHNICAL DATA
MOS 6502 at 1.8 MHz, 8 KB RAM

ATARI 400

AVAILABLE
November 1979

MANUFACTURER
Atari Inc.

While the other pioneers of the early microcomputer industry built serious computers for offices and hobbyists, Atari was different. After all, Atari was a videogame pioneer, having released the first commercial videogame, *Computer Space*, in arcades; had the first commercial success, with *Pong*; and, in 1977, released the 2600 console, which went on to sell several million units.

Knowing how to appeal to mass audiences – and the importance of games – Atari's first full-blown computers, the 400 and 800, mixed plug-and-play simplicity with the technical know-how the company had gained since its founding in 1972. They dispensed with exposed circuit boards and command lines, instead using cartridges to hold programs, as the 2600 and the Exidy Sorcerer P. 39 did. Their ports had different shapes so users couldn't plug the wrong thing into the wrong place. And if there was no program loaded, they would go into a built-in Memo Pad text-editor mode rather than a confusing command line.

In a mark of the attitudes of the industry at the time, the proto-400 and -800 were codenamed Candy and Colleen after secretaries who worked at Atari. Candy was the games machine and Colleen the computer, but the differences between the two were largely down to marketing and extensibility. The 400 had two external expansion slots and one cartridge slot compared to the 800's four and one, and the 800 featured RGB video output. They

had the same processor and standard memory, and they shared the same Color Television Interface Adaptor (CTIA) and Alphanumeric Television Interface Controller (ANTIC) to power graphics and text video modes. The 400, however, featured a membrane keyboard, which was cheaper to manufacture and could survive the stickiest and crumbiest fingers, and its angular, wedge-shaped casing conjured a cleanly futuristic feel that contrasted with the more muted simplicity of the 800.

And of course both machines could play Atari's games. Most of its classics were ported to them, including *Centipede*, *Defender*, *Donkey Kong*, and *Missile Command*, as well as many licensed titles, from *Pac-Man* to *M.U.L.E.* Atari had made a gaming computer that it would build on for the next decade P. 129.

ORIGIN
United Kingdom

TECHNICAL DATA
National Semiconductor SC/MP,
256 B RAM

AVAILABLE
June 1978

MANUFACTURER
Science of Cambridge

SCIENCE OF CAMBRIDGE MK 14

The MK 14 marked the beginning of one of the most important dynasties in computing, headed by entrepreneur and inventor Clive Sinclair. A simplistic kit computer with exposed calculator innards, it was bare-bones to an extreme, but it was built with the same key value as Sinclair's other successful electronics: it was extremely cheap.

Like so many early microcomputer trailblazers, Clive Sinclair had previously built calculators, starting in 1972 at Sinclair Radionics with the Executive. With a red LED display and a slim black casing, it was the first calculator that truly fit in a pocket, its size the result of canny engineering that allowed it to run on tiny hearing-aid batteries. The Executive sold well and more models followed, but bankruptcy loomed when Sinclair attempted to market a digital watch plagued by technical issues. Sinclair Radionics was saved in 1976 by the UK's National Enterprise Board, which bought a 43 per cent stake, and Sinclair resigned in 1978.

He had another company on the side. He had asked long-time employee Chris Curry to run a startup called Science of Cambridge. In 1977, Curry, who would later cofound Acorn Computers P. 47, was looking for products to sell and met an engineer called Ian Williamson who had designed a kit microcomputer. It was equipped with a National Semiconductor SC/MP microprocessor, which was commonly used by experimentally minded enthusiasts, and a calculator keypad and display. Curry immediately drew up a contract to buy the design, which Williamson signed. But it was never countersigned: Sinclair blocked the deal because National Semiconductor, having seen the design and jumped on the opportunity to sell more products, had offered a package deal of its cheapest components that replaced Williamson's design. Sinclair was determined to keep the kit's price down, and Williamson found himself pushed out of what became the MK 14.

At £39.95, the MK 14 was cheaper than any other computer on the UK market – five times cheaper than the Nascom 1 and Compukit UK101 – and it sold 15,000 units, despite its low power, kit form, scrappy manual, and notoriously unreliable keypad. With Curry and Sinclair now seasoned microcomputer makers, the scene was set for Science of Cambridge, soon to be renamed Sinclair Computers and then Sinclair Research, to kickstart the British computer industry P. 48.

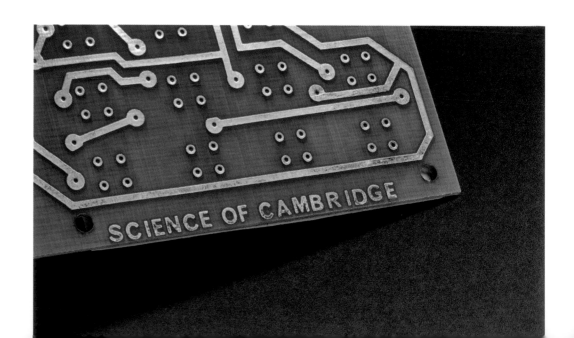

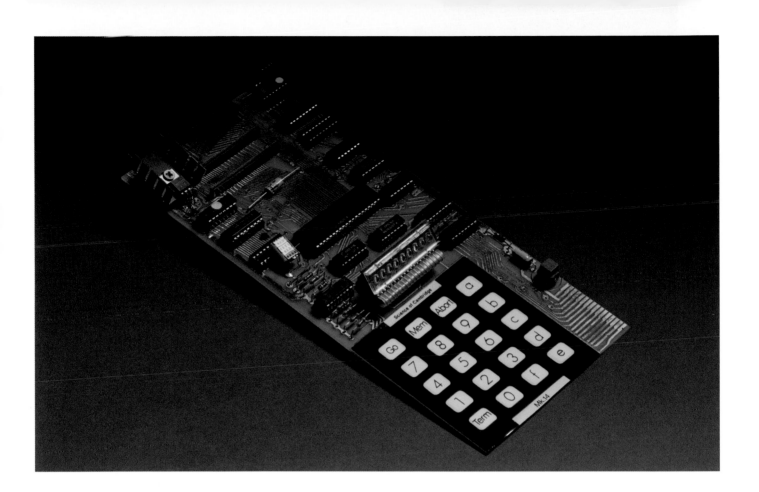

MANUFACTURER
Research Machines

AVAILABLE
February 1978

TECHNICAL DATA
Zilog Z80 at 4 MHz, 56 KB RAM maximum

ORIGIN
United Kingdom

With its tank-like metal case, the 380Z was built for the most demanding of environments: classrooms. There it flourished for years thanks to a design that was built for expansion, with floppy-disk drives, graphics cards, extra memory, and interfaces for new devices, enabling it to go on to serve new generations of children for many more years than its peers.

The 380Z came out of the kind of serendipity that was common in the early computer industry. Two graduates, Mike O'Regan and Mike Fischer, had founded a company in the early 1970s to make electronics products (they called it Research Machines because it sounded weighty, like International Business Machines), and moved into selling digital clock kits and components with a subsidiary business called Sintel. When they saw the Altair P. 22, they decided to make a computer themselves. They managed to sell 250, but the company got stuck, not big enough to grow. Until, that is, a couple of customers to whom Sintel had been selling electronics components approached O'Regan and Fischer. The men were trying to design a computer for schools, and they wondered if Sintel would create it.

O'Regan and Fischer jumped, and Fischer designed what became the 380Z in his bedroom. His philosophy was that no expense should be spared, because by the time the computer came out prices would have come down, and that it would be a working computer, not just for tinkerers. His ideas were exactly what schools were looking for. Both Bill Tagg, an influential figure in education who bought computers for Hertfordshire council, and Derek Esterson, who bought computers for inner London schools, were quick to back the 380Z, and the great majority of the 10,000 to 15,000 machines that Research Machines sold until 1985 were for education.

It was natural that Research Machines was invited to pitch for the BBC's microcomputer P. 72, but the company didn't like the tender: it demanded too many features, too low a price, and too little time to make it. Research Machines, after all, was in the business of making machines for the long haul P. 98.

RESEARCH MACHINES 380Z

ORIGIN
United Kingdom

TECHNICAL DATA
Rockwell 6502 at 1 MHz, 1 KB RAM

AVAILABLE
April 1979

MANUFACTURER
Acorn Computers

ACORN
SYSTEM 1

The MK 14's P.42 success convinced Chris Curry to develop it further as a computer system, but he found himself blocked by Science of Cambridge's owner, Clive Sinclair. Frustrated, Curry met with a friend called Hermann Hauser and decided to leave Sinclair. So began a long feud between the two figures who founded the British computer industry.

Hauser had recently finished his physics PhD and founded a company called Cambridge Processor Unit (CPU). His first commissions were controllers for fruit machines, but he had big ambitions. One idea was an 'electronic pocket book' that he was discussing with Sophie Wilson, a Cambridge maths undergraduate who made computer systems in her spare time. She had made a circuit for Cambridge Processor Unit that stopped thieves using lighters to trigger fruit machine payouts, and while talking through designs for Hauser's pocket book, she showed him her plans for a full 6502-powered computer based on a cow feeder she had been commissioned to make the previous summer.

That plan, which came together over the summer of 1978 as Wilson drew circuit boards on her parents' dining room table, became the Acorn System 1. The final machine comprised two circuit boards based on the Eurocard standard, one with a 6502 microprocessor and the other with a 25-button keypad, a nine-LED display, and a cassette interface.

In November, Hauser set up a company called Acorn Computers to sell the computer – its name intended to evoke the idea of expanding and growing – and the first kits shipped in April 1979. The team packed them in boxes themselves, standing around tables loaded with each component, and took the inevitable calls from customers who complained their kits did not work. It was a success, selling not only to laboratories and engineers but also to enthusiasts, and it even featured in the British sci-fi series *Blake's Seven* as a spaceship's control panel. Acorn Computers had emerged, and the next computer was only months away P.51.

ORIGIN
United Kingdom

TECHNICAL DATA
Zilog Z80 at 3.25 MHz, 1 KB RAM

AVAILABLE
January 1980

MANUFACTURER
Science of Cambridge

In 1978, the UK government watched the rise of the PET P. 28 and Apple II P. 31 and realized the history of the microcomputer was being written in the US. It was time to sponsor the development of a machine that could spur home-grown industry, and as it happened, the National Enterprise Board had a perfect manufacturer in its back pocket. It tasked Sinclair Radionics, in which it had bought a stake, with a project called the NewBrain.

To Clive Sinclair, however, the NewBrain was doomed to failure. He knew what it would take to inspire the revolution the project wanted to stimulate: a micro-computer that cost under £100. He reached his goal two years later in the form of the ZX80, after resigning from Sinclair Radionics. At £79.95 for a kit and £99.95 for a pre-assembled model, at launch the ZX80 was the cheapest computer ever released in the UK. Manufactured by Sinclair's new company, Science of Cambridge P. 42, it was named for the Z80 microprocessor that ran inside it, with the 'X' standing for 'the mystery ingredient', according to Rick Dickinson, who designed its futurist white exterior and integrated pressure-sensitive keyboard.

The insides were engineered by Jim Westwood, who developed many Sinclair computers and calculators. The ZX80 was a marvel of low-cost design, including a display technique that only output its black-and-white image when the processor was idle, causing the screen to flicker when pressing keys. It also stored the screen display in its 1 KB of RAM, leaving very little space to store programs. The ZX80 was the first in a run of Sinclair-branded microcomputers that squeezed low-cost production together with mass appeal. Sales reached around 50,000, but it was only on the market for a year. Ever restless, Sinclair was anxious to bring in a successor that would prove even more successful P. 71. The NewBrain, meanwhile, wasn't launched until 1982. Too late and too costly at £229, it couldn't live up to Sinclair's vision.

SINCLAIR ZX80

MANUFACTURER
Acorn Computers

AVAILABLE
February 1980

TECHNICAL DATA
MOS 6502 at 1 MHz, 2 KB RAM

ORIGIN
United Kingdom

ACORN BUS EXTENSION

ACORN COMPUTER CAMBRIDGE ENGLAND

VIA   PRINTER   I/O

VIDEO

The Acorn System 1 P. 47 went on to spawn a series of progressively more powerful kit computers, but Chris Curry was becoming increasingly keen to steer the company in a new direction. Clive Sinclair was working on a home computer, despite having stopped Curry from developing the MK 14 P. 42 when they worked together, and Curry wondered what it would mean to put a System-series computer in an attractive case.

Not everyone at Acorn believed in making computers for the volatile and price-sensitive home market; the company was doing just fine catering to laboratories and enthusiasts. But Hauser supported the idea, and work began on designing a new home computer based on the System 3. The Atom had less RAM and no disk drive, but it featured a full-size keyboard and it was designed to launch at a competitive price of £120 for the kit. Curry approached product designer Allen Boothroyd to design its case.

Inside the box was a copy of its manual, *Atomic Theory and Practice*, which was written by David Johnson-Davies, who went on to found in-house software publisher AcornSoft later in 1980. This was the book that taught *Elite* co-creator David Braben to code, after having been given an Atom for Christmas as his first computer. In fact, as testament to the Atom's extensibility, the first prototypes of *Elite*, which was written for the BBC Micro, were coded on one.

Selling 20,000 units, the Atom was the most successful Acorn computer yet, and something of a provocation towards Sinclair's ZX80 P. 48, which launched only a few weeks before it. The Atom was rather more expensive, but had colour graphics, a full keyboard, and more RAM, and it provided its fans with plenty of reasons to sneer. At Acorn, however, the team was becoming pretty tired of selling kit computers, having to pack the components themselves, and taking calls from customers who had decided to assemble their Atoms with glue because they thought soldering would damage them. The next computer would widen Acorn's horizons considerably P. 72.

ACORN ATOM

MANUFACTURER
Tandy Corporation

AVAILABLE
September 1983

TECHNICAL DATA
Motorola MC6809E at 0.89 MHz, 16 KB or
64 KB RAM

ORIGIN
United States

RADIO SHACK TRS-80 COLOR COMPUTER 2

While the TRS-80 P. 27 helped to define the low-cost computer in Radio Shacks across the US, Tandy was also interested in building computers for workplaces. In 1977, it started a project with Motorola to design a computer terminal that displayed important agricultural information for farmers, which was updated hourly over a phone line. The AgVision used a Motorola MC6808 microprocessor and MC6847 video processor for colour output, but although trial units were distributed in Kentucky in 1978, it proved too expensive to go into full production.

However, the following year Motorola squeezed many of its chips into a single multiplexer and replaced its CPU with the newer MC6809. Tandy revisited the design and released, in 1980, the TRS-80 Videotex, a terminal that could connect to general information servers ('Imagine having a public library that never closes right in your home or office!')

It didn't take much to convert the Videotex into a full computer. Tandy took out its modem and added cartridge and interface slots, called it the TRS-80 Color Computer, and sold it as a serious computer for homes at $399 in July 1980, alongside the TRS-80 Model III. Since the CoCo, as it became known,

had no technical relationship with the original TRS-80, it didn't support any of its software, but its four-colour display made it stand out above all the black-and-white computers around it and it inspired various clones, such as the Dragon 32 P. 95 and the Laser 200 P. 138.

The CoCo may have been ugly, but it was much loved by its owners and was revised many times over the following years, including an upgrade to Extended Color BASIC, which added powerful new graphics commands, and more RAM. In 1983, Tandy released the Color Computer 2, which was smaller and featured a much-improved keyboard and more RAM. Although the Commodore 64 P. 79 was available for less, Tandy's national reach, through Radio Shack's catalogues and stores, maintained the CoCo's appeal so that it just kept on going. In 1986 Tandy released a third version, which was sold all the way up until 1991.

ORIGIN
United States

TECHNICAL DATA
MOS 6502 at 1 MHz / MOS 6560,
5 KB RAM

AVAILABLE
October 1980

MANUFACTURER
Commodore Business Machines

Commodore had spearheaded the personal computer with the PET P. 28, but with competition beginning to rise, Jack Tramiel asked MOS to design a successor. Rather portentously called The Other Intellect (TOI), the project didn't work out; its design was too demanding for the hardware of the time. So when Tramiel learned that MOS engineer Robert Yannes had been designing a computer called the MicroPET in his spare time, he immediately asked for it to go into production. It would eventually become the Vic-20.

True to its name, the MicroPET was not a next-generation computer – and that's why Commodore liked it. During TOI's development, Tramiel had noticed that microcomputers were beginning to appeal to a new kind of customer: an extremely price-conscious one. But Tramiel believed the PET's successor would need to display colours so it could compete with the TRS-80 Color Computer P. 53 and Atari 400 P. 40, while also keeping up with Tramiel's belief that Japanese computers were about to flood the market P. 63. After all, he had plenty of experience of being overtaken by new Japanese technology.

MOS chip designer Al Charpentier developed the VIC, the Video Interface Chip, which was specially designed to handle graphics and sound processing. It could display sixteen colours across a native 176-by-184-pixel resolution, and it featured three channels of square-wave sound and one channel of white noise. The VIC-20, therefore, could play games, a feature Commodore capitalized on by commissioning text-adventure maker Scott Adams to convert five of his games to the new machine. The first production run went on to generate $1.5 million in revenue. Indeed, titles such as Jeff Minter's *Gridrunner*, Ron Haliburton's *Omega Race*, and Jeff McCord's *Sword of Fargoal* became a vital part of the VIC-20's success: by the end of its first year in production it had become the first computer to sell over a million units, and it would soon be at the centre of a vicious price war that would remodel the entire market.

COMMODORE VIC-20

ORIGIN
United States

TECHNICAL DATA
HP 8-bit processor at 0.61 MHz,
16 KB RAM

AVAILABLE
January 1980

MANUFACTURER
Hewlett-Packard

HEWLETT-PACKARD HP-85

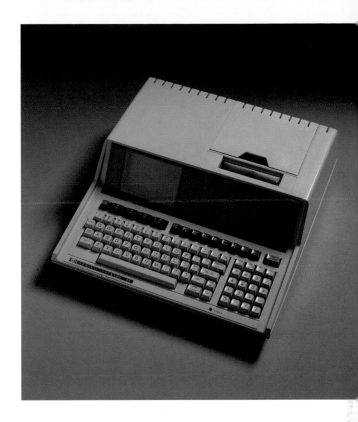

As the programmable calculator evolved into the personal computer, it was often difficult to define the difference between them. Hewlett-Packard's 1972 HP 9830 featured a full keyboard and a BASIC interpreter, and yet HP referred to it as a calculator. In fact, Steve Wozniak, who joined HP in 1973 and would go on to design the Apple I and II P. 81, was rebuffed in 1976 when he tried to suggest that HP created a computer. But towards the end of the decade HP realized that things had changed, and it marketed its HP-85 as a personal computer, even if it took a similar form to the 9800 range, packing every necessary component into a slightly smaller case, exchanging the 9800's LED display for a 5-in. CRT one, and adding a built-in thermal printer.

Despite its uncertain heritage, the HP-85 was HP's bid to build the leading computer platform. Almost everything inside it was proprietary, designed and built by HP itself, right down to its microprocessor. HP had learned a thing or two from building calculators, particularly the importance of accuracy. The common early microprocessors could only spit out solutions to calculations as inaccurate whole numbers. HP, on the other hand, made calculators that did their arithmetic in binary-coded decimal, accurate to 12 decimal places. The process was slower – the HP-85's microprocessor ran at one-sixth the number of cycles of a Z80 – but, HP surmised, the future of computing would align with accuracy rather than brute speed. Besides, being capable of performing more operations per cycle than other processors, the HP-85 could run programs just as fast.

HP's gamble didn't pay off, of course. The main issue with creating a unique architecture was that every piece of software needed to be completely re-written for the HP-85. HP believed that the problem would be short-lived, surmising that programming would turn to standard high-level languages such as C, which could simply compile to different processor architectures. In reality, the processors that evolved from Intel's 8008, from the Z80 to the 6502, would take precedence, and HP would have to follow suit.

ORIGIN
United States

TECHNICAL DATA
Synertek 6502A at 1.8 MHz, 128 KB RAM

AVAILABLE
May 1980

MANUFACTURER
Apple Computer

APPLE III

Apple rode high on the success of the Apple II , but not quite for the reasons Steve Wozniak expected. It proved particularly successful among businesses, rather than the homes he thought it would sell into. Businesses liked the Disk II floppy-disk drive, which was released in 1978, and they loved VisiCalc, the first spreadsheet. Designed specifically for the Apple II by programmer Dan Bricklin while he was at Harvard Business School, and released in 1979, VisiCalc presented a completely novel way of using a computer, using its computational power to display and manipulate numbers, and it quickly caught on. Over the following year, VisiCalc was ported to all the leading computer systems of the time, but it led with the Apple II version. Across six years it sold over 700,000 copies at a price that started at $100 per copy.

Seeing the Apple II's sales, Apple decided to design a more powerful computer that was more focused on business needs. It featured a faster 6502-based processor and could access more memory than the 6502 could normally manage, all the way up to 128 KB, and it featured a floppy-disk drive. Its fuller keyboard, which incorporated a number pad and cursor keys, could type upper- and lower-case characters, all the better for writing documents and navigating VisiCalc tables.

It sounded good on paper, but the Apple III was a failure. Its power came with a very high price – $4,340 for the cheapest model – and Apple had to recall the first 14,000 units due to logic-board failures. Steve Jobs had demanded another fanless and ventless case, and the heat buildup inside tended to warp the logic board, loosening chips. Further, its real-time clock would fail over time, and although it shipped with an emulator to run Apple II software, it was restricted to emulating the 48-KB version. Most seriously, it contravened US radio frequency emission regulations. Apple issued two revised models, the IIIs and the Plus, over the next three years, but the Apple III was never adopted as widely as the II: it only sold 120,000 units.

Apple III, keyboard, detail ↑

MANUFACTURER
Sharp Corporation

AVAILABLE
December 1978

TECHNICAL DATA
Sharp Z80 at 2 MHz, 20 KB RAM

ORIGIN
Japan

As the company that developed the first transistor-powered calculator (the CS-10A, in 1964) and the first LCD pocket calculator (the EL-805, in 1973), Sharp was well placed to join the computer revolution. But this massive maker of hi-fis and TVs took tentative steps. Its MZ-40K single-board kit computer did not emerge until May 1978, and for most hobbyists it was more toy than serious machine; its built-in software included games and an organ that played notes through its integrated speaker. However, it laid the foundations for one of the first hits of the early Japanese home computer market.

The MZ-80K was an all-in-one computer designed along the same philosophical lines as the big American home computers, the Apple II **P.31**, PET **P.28**, and TRS-80 **P.53**. It featured a built-in monochrome display and keyboard, and a tape drive for storage that was rated at 1200 bauds – four times the speed of common tape players. But it didn't ship with a ROM loaded with an operating system: instead, one had to be loaded from tape. This was a key way in which Sharp was able to reduce costs, but the company marketed it as a feature called 'Clean Design': your computer came to you fresh and free of bugs. It lent the machine flexibility, if not convenience; it supported many different languages, including BASIC, Pascal, and FORTRAN, produced by software developers such as Japan-based Hudson and ASCII.

The MZ-80K was never released on the US market, but it found some success in Europe, despite not amassing a great deal of software – although many games were made for it in Japan – and being equipped with an awkwardly laid out keyboard (which was a lot higher quality than the one in the first PET). This was partly because the MZ-80K was comparatively cheap: in 1980, a 36-KB model was advertised at £423, while a PET with 32 KB cost £600. In Japan, though, its only rival was NEC's PC-8001, and it spawned a long-running series of computers with the MZ badge, including the MZ-700 **P.102** and the graphics-based MZ-80B.

SHARP MZ-80K

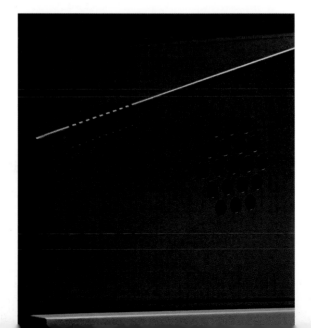

ORIGIN
United States

TECHNICAL DATA
Zilog Z80 at 4 MHz, 64 KB RAM

AVAILABLE
April 1981

MANUFACTURER
Osborne Computer Corporation

OSBORNE 1

It was all very well having to keep computers chained to the desk, but sooner or later they had to be made portable. And the first personal computer that came with every necessary component integrated into a single housing was the Osborne 1. Designed to fit under an airliner passenger seat, it looked like a boxy suitcase with a leather carrying handle. But if you were to crack it open, it would reveal a full keyboard, two floppy-disk drives, a number of ports and interfaces, and a minute 5-in. screen: everything you needed for some computing, if you could find a power outlet and squint.

It wasn't pretty; it weighed 11 kg (24 lb); the screen could only display five lines of text at a time; and it cost $1,795. But the Osborne 1 came with a suite of bundled software that was tailor-made for business use, including WordStar P. 109, a spreadsheet called SuperCalc, Microsoft's MBASIC, and Digital Research's CBASIC, which Osborne secured for the machine by offering their makers stock in the company. Later Osborne offered dBase II with the machine, causing such a run on supply that manufacturing couldn't keep up. The value of the software alone was enough to make the Osborne 1 an attractive deal to businesses.

And yet it was Osborne's only computer. Despite strong sales of over 125,000 units in 1982, in autumn 1983 the company went bankrupt. Earlier in the year, founder Adam Osborne had announced two new models, the Executive and Vixen, emphasizing just how much more powerful they would be than the Osborne 1. From the outside, it seemed that his braggadocio caused dealers to suddenly withdraw their orders for the 1 because they knew something better was on the near horizon. The idea that it was all Osborne's fault became so strongly held that the term 'Osborne effect' was coined to mean the phenomenon of a premature product announcement killing interest in existing products. However, Osborne's employees blamed competition with new portable computers such as the cheaper Kaypro II, which came with a larger monitor; the growing appeal of IBM's 5150 P. 66; and the severe problems that came with growing the company so quickly to satisfy demand.

Osborne 1, cable tray ↑

ORIGIN
United States

TECHNICAL DATA
Intel 8088 at 4.77 MHz, 16 KB–256 KB RAM

AVAILABLE
August 1981

MANUFACTURER
IBM

The year before IBM launched the 5150, its cheapest computer cost $13,000. This behemoth of a company had never sold a product through retailers before, and rumours persisted that every internal decision took weeks of meetings. Its staff even had to wear suits and ties. What could it possibly bring to the exploding microcomputer market? Its answer was the PC, a freely extensible computer made from standardized parts that would eventually unify a field of splintered and proprietary platforms.

Onlookers were right to doubt IBM's ability to make the 5150, because in order for its design team, led by Don Estridge, to take it from concept to launch in just twelve months, it had to break all IBM's internal rules. The 5150's microprocessor was Intel's 8088, not IBM's own, far more powerful, 801 RISC processor. Its operating system was Microsoft's DOS 1.0. It shipped with Microsoft's popular BASIC, not IBM's own flavour of the language. Its memory, monitor, and printer circuit boards were off-the-shelf models, sourced through a bidding process that pitted IBM's own hardware divisions against external companies. And the 5150's architecture was open, so anyone could understand how it worked and develop their own software and peripherals for it, just as they could with the Apple II P.31. One of the few parts of the computer that was IBM's own was its ROM BIOS, the 5150's core firmware.

With aggressive pricing, a suite of business-oriented software including the Apple II-boosting VisiCalc, and a massive IBM marketing push, the 5150 took 40,000 orders on its first day. Over the following few years a burgeoning ecosystem of software and peripherals grew, which compounded its early success, and the 5150 became known simply as the IBM PC. The era of the personal computer was born. Little did IBM know that its ownership of the world's leading computer format would be so short-lived P.120.

IBM 5150

ORIGIN
United States

TECHNICAL DATA
TI TMS9900 at 3 MHz, 256 B scratchpad
RAM and 16 KB graphics RAM

AVAILABLE
June 1981

MANUFACTURER
Texas Instruments

TEXAS INSTRUMENTS
TI-99/4A

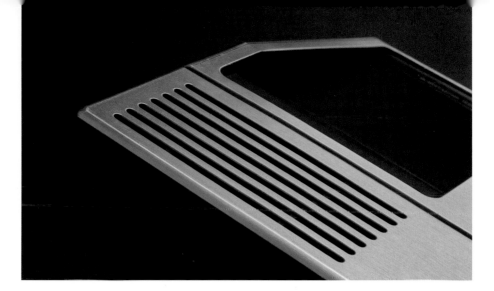

Just as the HP-85 **P. 59** bore the legacy of the calculators that preceded it, so too did Texas Instruments' first computer, the TI-99/4. Featuring a chiclet keyboard and lacking lower-case characters and a graphics mode, it even offered to start up its equation mode when it booted up. But it was, nevertheless, a full computer with a 16-bit CPU and a large monitor, and TI hoped it would compete with the PET **P. 28**, Apple II **P. 31**, and TRS-80 **P. 27** when it launched in 1979. But it didn't do particularly well, especially since it came with a whopping price tag of $1,150.

But with the 1981 release of its revision, the 4A, the machine's fortunes turned around. It sported a new graphics chip, supported lower-case characters (well, in the form of small uppercase letters), and, most importantly, it cost $525 without a monitor. TI realized price was everything, and the next year it reduced the 4A again to just $200 after a $100 rebate. That placed it below the VIC-20 **P. 56**, which was retailing at $300. With the simultaneous appearance of the Timex Sinclair 1000 **P. 124**, a price war erupted. Commodore slashed the VIC-20's price to $200 in time for Christmas, to just $130 in January 1983, and to a mere $100 in April. By the end of spring, the 4A was also $100, and TI was making a loss on each sale. It even cut the price of software and add-on hardware, the products that should have been generating the profit – all to make the 4A more attractive than any other computer.

Commodore, however, was in a better place to wage the war. With its own engineering and fabrication facilities, it could better reduce costs, while TI relied on buying components from third parties. In October 1983, TI posted $111 million in losses and announced it would be withdrawing the 4A. Retailers began selling their remaining inventory for just $50. The price war, which hit at the same time as the videogame crash, rocked the low-cost computer industry to its core.

MANUFACTURER
Sinclair Research

AVAILABLE
March 1981

TECHNICAL DATA
Z80 at 3.25 MHz, 1 KB RAM

ORIGIN
United Kingdom

Compare the ZX81 with the ZX80  P.48 that preceded it, and other than its new low-cut black casing, there's very little to tell between them. Inside was the same microprocessor and 1 KB of RAM, though it could be upgraded to 64 KB. Look closer and you might notice that the ZX81 had just four chips, and the ROM, into which Sinclair BASIC was squeezed, was doubled to 8 KB. But these were minor changes compared to the tag on its box. The ZX80's sub-£100 price broke the rules for home computers, but the ZX81 slashed off a further £30. It was enough to convince John Rowland of nationwide high-street retailer WH Smith to strike an exclusive deal. WH Smith was the first mainstream UK shop to stock a microcomputer, and Sinclair went on to sell over one and a half million of them.

Engineer Jim Westwood had managed another feat of cost-saving. He had replaced eighteen individual chips in the ZX80 with a single uncommitted logic array, a special multi-function chip that meant Sinclair didn't need to design and commission its own custom one. Industrial designer Rick Dickinson had retained the ZX80's membrane keyboard, but since its forty keys could have up to five different functions, he had to cram notation for each into every key. Together with the casing, it won him a British Design Council award.

But the real heroes of the ZX81 were John Grant and Steve Vickers, who recrafted Sinclair BASIC for its larger ROM. They added floating-point calculations – the ZX80 didn't support fractions or decimals – which expanded its practicality, and they created a function that checked for errors in code as it was entered, rather than when it was run. This detail was essential for new programmers, who would usually also be following Vickers' comprehensive manual, *ZX81 BASIC Programming*. Sinclair and its marketing company highlighted the ZX81 as an introduction to computers, and they were right. This was the machine that first introduced programming to the masses of Britain and beyond.

SINCLAIR ZX81

ACORN BBC MICROCOMPUTER MODEL A

ORIGIN
United Kingdom

TECHNICAL DATA
MOS 6502 at 2 MHz, 16 KB RAM

AVAILABLE
December 1981

MANUFACTURER
Acorn Computers

In the late 1970s, the British government became increasingly concerned that the UK was lagging behind the rise of the microcomputer, with businesses slow to take up new ways of working and a culture slow to understand what was already transforming countries such as the US. When the British TV channel ITV began to broadcast a five-part series called *The Mighty Micro* in October 1979, it proved tremendously influential in government circles and helped to persuade the British Broadcasting Corporation (BBC) to establish the Computer Literacy Project. This educational initiative, led by Sheila Innes and supported by the Department of Trade and Industry, would spearhead national awareness of how to use computers through a series of TV programmes, and would be supported by an associated computer.

Acorn had risen as a microcomputer manufacturer P. 51, but it was still tiny compared to Sinclair. Securing the commission to design and build that computer would surely lead to huge sales. Clive Sinclair had the same idea, of course, but the BBC's specification was demanding, requiring that the machine demonstrate programming, sound, music, graphics, teletext, and even artificial intelligence. Acorn had been working on a new microcomputer design codenamed Proton, but it was all still on paper, so the design team, led by Steve Furber, had just a week to get a prototype running to demonstrate to the BBC.

The ploy worked, and the deal was done. One important task for engineer Sophie Wilson was to write BBC BASIC, the full-featured, fast, and yet accessible language that came installed on the BBC Micro's ROM, sealing its use as a programming tool. The BBC connection ensured it was bought by every school in the country. But while practical, the BBC Micro eked the very most out of its 6502 and was great for games, home to technical showcases such as *Elite* and *Exile*. The solace for Sinclair was that although BBC Micro launched at £235, production costs required it to be raised by £60 soon afterwards, so there was plenty of room to undercut it with a cheaper machine. It helped, too, that the BBC Micro never quite shifted its air of being a computer for teacher's pet.

ower output
1·25A
DC @ 1·25A
5V DC @ 75ma.

Industrial design by Allen Boothroyd
Assembled in United Kingdom.

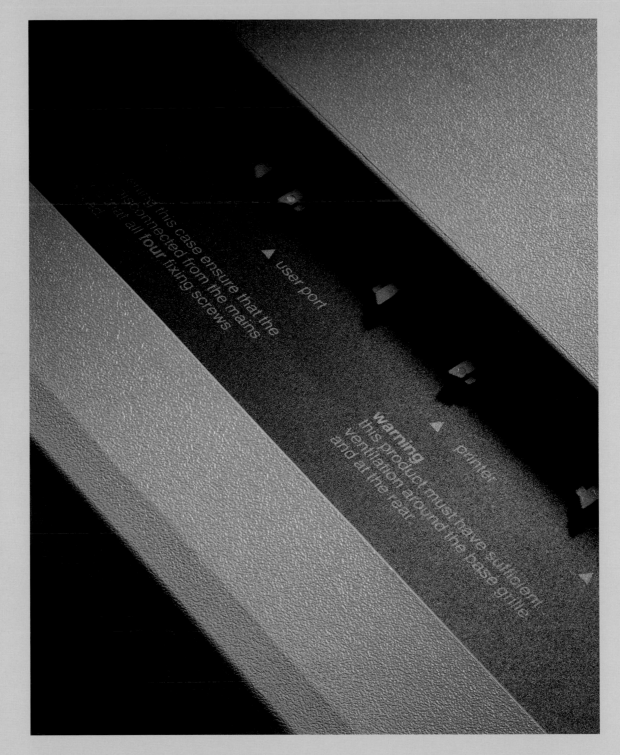

this case ensure that the
disconnected from the mains
all four fixing screws

▲ user port

warning
this product must have sufficient
ventilation around the base grille
and at the rear

▲ printer

MANUFACTURER
EACA

AVAILABLE
1981

TECHNICAL DATA
Zilog Z80 at 1.76 MHz, 16 KB RAM

ORIGIN
Hong Kong

EG 3008

Eric Chung grew up in mainland China, but he managed to cross the border into Hong Kong, which was then a British colony. Legend says that he spent his first night in the city sleeping in a railway station, but before long he had founded a small electronics empire called EACA. Among the products it made were radios and *Pong*-style TV games, as well as the Video Genie series of computers.

The first to make it to market was the Video Genie System in early 1980. Heavily based on the TRS-80 **P.27** and featuring the same Z80A microprocessor, it was followed by the Genie I, which supported lower-case characters. The Genie II, which was released in 1981, exchanged the original machine's integrated tape recorder for a keypad so it could be marketed as a business computer. The Colour Genie EG 2000, released in August 1982, was a little more ambitious, ditching compatibility with the TRS-80 and previous Video Genies in favour of better graphics support, a Z80 running at a faster clock speed, and three-channel sound. Its graphics mode was too low-resolution for text, however, so it couldn't hold a candle to the more popular 8-bit systems of its time, such as the ZX Spectrum **P.91**, and it lacked software support.

The Genie systems were distributed across the world by different companies. In Europe they were handled by EACA and local distributors, while in Australasia they were handled by the retailer Dick Smith Electronics and known as the Dick Smith System 80. In North America they were managed by Personal Micro Computers (PMC), which sold the Genie II as the PMC 81. Tandy took PMC to court, claiming PMC infringed a copyright Tandy held for its ROM I/O routines, and won – but worse was to come for EACA. Chung had been speculating in Hong Kong property with the company's finances and had fallen on bad fortune, and in October 1983 EACA abruptly went bankrupt. Despite some of EACA's electronics lines struggling in the marketplace, most staff were entirely unaware of any problems, and legend has it that as they woke up to the news, Chung was fleeing Hong Kong for Taiwan with a suitcase stuffed with millions of dollars.

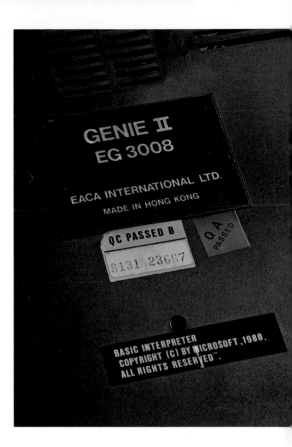

EACA GENIE II EG 3008

MANUFACTURER
Commodore International

AVAILABLE
August 1982

TECHNICAL DATA
MOS 6510 at 1 MHz, 64 KB RAM

ORIGIN
United States

COMMODORE 64

The Commodore 64 was both a rush job and the most successful computer of its generation, capturing the minds of children, programmers, artists, and engineers alike. Its combination of shrewd economy and future-gazing technology would see it dominate the market and remain in production until 1994.

But it didn't come directly from a plan to build a computer. In January 1981, casting around for a new project to work on, Commodore's chip engineers at MOS decided to make a console that would bring about the next generation of video-games. Knowing it had to be cheap, they designed a new microprocessor based on MOS's own 6502. They calculated a die size that would result in economic yields, added an extra I/O port, gave it access to more RAM, and called it the 6510. So far, so prudent.

But alongside the 6510 grew two new chips. MOS's team, led by Al Charpentier and Charles Winterble, looked at the Intellivision console, TI-99 P-99, and Atari 800 P-40, and designed the VIC-II 6567 video chip to match and exceed them. It featured sprites and collision detection support, 320-by-200-pixel resolution, and a native palette of sixteen colours.

And then there was the SID 6581 sound chip. Designer Robert Yannes brought his appreciation of electronic music to chip engineering and produced by far the most advanced sound hardware yet available in a home computer. The SID could simultaneously play three synthesized voices, and its envelope generator could control the volume, pitch, and frequency of each as it played. The SID gave soon-to-be-famous game music composers such as Rob Hubbard and Martin Galway a true instrument to program, rich with nuance for individual style and expression.

The chips were completed in November 1981, prompting Commodore CEO Jack Tramiel to order the team to complete the 64's design for display at the CES expo in just six weeks' time. If they had had longer, perhaps the SID could have been even better: Yannes was planning for thirty-two independent voices. But it was certainly enough.

Personal Computer

IBM
Personal Computers

Guide to Operations

As computers and software took on a wider variety of roles in both home and business life, their packaging and manuals reflected this by becoming more expressive. Those for home computers began to be suggestive of the households in which they would be found, the people who would use them, and the things that they would make. Products created for business aimed for a greater sense of prestige. Computers and packages such as VisiCalc had earned a new position in the office, and their users expected them to exhibit a fitting air of professionalism.

IBM PC 5150 *Guide to Operations* manual

Sam Coupé packaging

Acorn

Apple IIe Owner's Manual

Acorn Archimendes RISC OS 3 user and
applications guide

Acorn Electron packaging

Sinclair ZX Spectrum 128K packaging

acorn electron

ZX Spectrum 128

Personal Computer

Peter Rodwell

Covers the complete range including the Apricot XEN

HEINEMANN
NEW TECH

TOSHIBA
HOME COMPUTER MODEL **HX-10**

MSX
64k

MEMOTECH

BASIC TUTOR, REFERENCE &
OPERATOR'S MANUAL

MTX
SERIES

*Introducing the Apricot
Business Computer*

Toshiba HX-10 packaging

BBC Micro welcome tape

MTX512 *Operator's Manual*

Tatung Einstein manual

Camputers Lynx *User Manual*

Science of Cambridge MK 14 *Training Manual*

VisiCalc software package

User
Instructions

AMSTRAD

MITS
"Creative Electronics"

ALTAIR
DOCUMENTATION

Rainbow 100™

MITS Altair 8800 *Documentation*

Amstrad PPC 512/640
User Instructions   DEC Rainbow 100 manual

digital

MANUFACTURER
Sinclair Research

AVAILABLE
April 1982

TECHNICAL DATA
Z80A at 3.5 MHz, 16 KB–48 KB RAM

ORIGIN
United Kingdom

SINCLAIR ZX SPECTRUM

The race to build a computer for the BBC was intense, and the loser, Sinclair Research, had to watch its rival P.72 being promoted across national TV screens. How could it continue to compete in the home computer market? Clive Sinclair's answer was, once again, about price. The ZX Spectrum was a marvel of cost-saving design by industrial designer Rick Dickinson and engineer Richard Altwasser, who had to engineer new solutions for almost every element, from its BASIC interpreter, which was squeezed into a 16-KB ROM, to its raised rubber keyboard, a development from those of the ZX80 P. 48 and ZX81 P. 71, but still only requiring four or five moving parts.

But Altwasser's memory conservation system was the Spectrum's cleverest and most distinctive property. For a machine that was named for its colour support, the Spectrum was very restrictive with it, only supporting fifteen in total: two shades of seven colours, plus black. But colour data wasn't stored with the pixel bitmaps you see on-screen. Instead, the Spectrum stored colour across the screen in a low-resolution grid of just thirty-two by twenty-four blocks. Each block, 8 by 8 pixels in size, held information for just two colours and whether they were set to flash, which rapidly alternated the foreground and background.

This was the reason for the Spectrum's unmistakable attribute clash, which caused a character walking across the screen to inherit, chameleon-like, the colours of the blocks behind it, and also why it couldn't display more than two colours next to each other unless they were in neighbouring blocks. It imposed a stern creative challenge on programmers and artists as they attempted to make great-looking games, but for Spectrum owners, attribute clash was simply part of what the machine was.

The result of these design choices was a home computer that cost half the price of a BBC Micro – and 30,000 backlogged orders three months after launch. The Spectrum soon became the UK's best-selling computer, inspiring a flowering of software (which is to say games, many made by children who learned to program through its command line). Arguably, the Spectrum did far more to educate a newly computer-literate generation than the computer it was designed to stand up to.

ORIGIN
United Kingdom

TECHNICAL DATA
Zilog Z80A at 3.25 MHz, 3 KB RAM

AVAILABLE
September 1982

MANUFACTURER
Jupiter Cantab

JUPITER
CANTAB ACE

Even as they worked on the ZX Spectrum P. 91, programmer Steve Vickers and hardware designer Richard Altwasser had another computer on their minds. After all, Sinclair was reaping great rewards for their work. Wasn't it about time that they used their skills to create their own machine? So, as soon as the Spectrum shipped in April 1982, they founded Rainbow Computing, the name Altwasser had wanted to give the Spectrum. Their idea was to exploit a niche they thought cheap computers weren't reaching: programmers and the technically minded. And although Vickers had lots of experience with BASIC from putting it into the ZX81 and Spectrum, they would base their computer on an entirely different language: Forth.

Forth ran a lot faster than BASIC did on Sinclair's machines, despite the ACE's Z80 running slightly slower than the Spectrum's. Vickers had written it so that the ACE converted into native code as it ran, and although the base model of the machine only had 3 KB of RAM, Forth wasn't nearly as memory-hungry as BASIC. What's more, Vickers believed that Forth was easier to learn than BASIC, making the ACE appealing for children. Not everyone agreed with him, partly because Forth was so different to the ubiquitous BASIC.

The pair named the machine the ACE after the Pilot ACE, an early computer that was built at the National Physical Laboratory where Vickers' father worked, and they renamed the company to honour the city in which it was designed, Cambridge. Small, white, and streamlined, ACE certainly had the looks. Given that Altwasser had designed Sinclair's computers, it's forgivable that it could have passed as a Sinclair machine, complete with rubber membrane keyboard.

But despite its low £89.95 launch price, the niche Vickers and Altwasser chose proved too small, and since they eschewed a graphics mode the ACE wasn't going to have the same appeal for children as the Spectrum. It didn't help that Altwasser and Vickers didn't manage to amass the ACE a strong library of games and software. Although they attempted to break into the US market the following year with an updated version, the ACE 4000, Jupiter Cantab went bankrupt in November with the ACE having sold between 5,000 and 8,000 units.

Jupiter Cantab ACE, UHF and tape sockets ↑

DRAGON 32

ORIGIN
United Kingdom

TECHNICAL DATA
Motorola MC6809E at 0.89 MHz,
32 KB RAM

AVAILABLE
August 1982

MANUFACTURER
Dragon Data

The early home computer industry was extraordinarily volatile, with companies sparking up, shining bright, and then burning out over the course of just a few months. But the computer revolution didn't just touch computer makers. Mettoy had made metal toys in the UK since the 1930s, and founded the tremendously successful Corgi range of model cars in the 1950s. But its management noticed that the rapid rise of computers was changing the way children played. If Mettoy wanted to stay relevant, they said, it should get into computers.

Project Sam kicked off in late 1981. Mettoy gave consultancy PA Technology a tight deadline to design a computer. Without time to write something tailored, the team licensed Microsoft BASIC, a decision that immediately restricted the range of microprocessors the computer could have. The design team looked to the Motorola 6809, which naturally fitted with Motorola's memory and video controller chips and was comfortably faster than the Z80 and 6502. It just happened that it also matched the configuration of the TRS-80 CoCo P. 53, which had successfully launched in the US the previous year, and thus took advantage of supporting a great deal of its software.

After a last-minute doubling of its RAM from 16 KB to 32 KB in order to keep up with new machines on the block, such as the Spectrum, the Dragon 32 was launched. Sales were brisk, but two months later Mettoy began to run into financial difficulties, which many blamed on its heavy investment in the Dragon. To save the computer, Dragon Data, initially a subsidiary, became a separate company just as Mettoy went into receivership.

It only delayed Dragon Data's demise. It took too long to release a promised follow-up, the Dragon 64, and the Spectrum, Commodore 64 P. 79, and BBC Micro P.72 claimed the market. Although the company continued to design prototypes for new machines, such as the dual-CPU, business-oriented Alpha, and the Dragon 32 and 64 were released in the US as the Tano Dragon, continuing difficulties saw Dragon Data being subsumed by General Electric Company in 1983. In 1984 it was sold off to a new Spanish firm called Eurohard, which collapsed, finally taking Dragon Data down too, in 1987.

ORIGIN
United Kingdom

TECHNICAL DATA
MOS 6502A at 1 MHz, 16 KB or
32 KB RAM

AVAILABLE
December 1982

MANUFACTURER
Oric Products International

ORIC-1

Every new computer faced a multitude of challenges if it tried to compete in the British home computer market of the early 1980s. The price had to be low. The manufacturing supply had to flow. It had to perform well. The games had to be good. At least Tangerine had plenty of experience with designing commercial computers, having released the cleverly engineered Microtan 65 kit for enthusiasts and scientists in 1979. So when its principal venture-capital funder, British Car Auctions, saw opportunity in investing in the exploding home market, Tangerine (yes, its name was inspired by Apple) formed a subsidiary called Oric Products International and set its sights on the ZX Spectrum P. 91.

In terms of price, the Oric-1 was right on track. At launch, its 16-KB model cost less than the Spectrum. It had a better keyboard. It had an existing magazine, the *Tansoft Gazette*, to help with promotion. Its innards were based on the already-proven Microtan, but it featured an advanced sound chip, the General Instruments 8912, which would later be used in the Atari ST, and although it suffered from attribute clash like the Spectrum, it was much less pronounced.

But what counted against the Oric-1 was its buggy BASIC ROM, which was written in Forth, then translated into machine code before being incorporated into the ROM. The work required months of debugging, and users still had trouble loading programs from cassette and from IF/THEN/ELSE statements that didn't work correctly. These setbacks helped delay the Oric-1's release, which was originally meant to be in October 1982, until December; advance units released to the press were broken and lacked documentation, leading to bad reviews. What's more, Oric couldn't build the Oric-1 as cheaply as it aimed, leading to a £30 price increase in May 1983. And then: disaster. On 13 October 1983, the factory where the Oric-1 was being built burned down, taking with it 7,000 finished systems and 15,000 ROM chips.

Still, in 1983, 160,000 Oric-1s were sold in the UK and 50,000 in France, where the Oric-1 was specifically designed to support the French SECAM TV standard. The figures were below Oric's target and the Spectrum still reigned supreme, but the Oric wasn't beaten yet P. 155.

ORIGIN
United Kingdom

TECHNICAL DATA
Zilog Z80A at 4 MHz, 32 KB–256 KB RAM

RESEARCH MACHINES LINK 480Z

AVAILABLE
1982

MANUFACTURER
Research Machines

Research Machines' 380Z P.45 was a workhorse of a school computer, which could grow as years of dependable service went by. But it was expensive, partly because of the storage add-ons each machine needed. So Research Machines had an idea: if every computer was networked together, perhaps they could all share one floppy or hard drive? That idea inspired the 480Z. Without the need to make space available for storage devices, Research Machines squeezed the 380Z's essentials under a full keyboard and released it for half the price. The 480Z could run as a standalone Microsoft BASIC-powered computer, or, by booting it to the CP/NOS operating system (a version of CP/M for networks), it could be connected to other machines and share data – hence the 'Link' in its name.

Although it was cut down from its bigger forebear, the 480Z's 32 KB of RAM was upgradable to 256 KB. Its Z80 microprocessor could only access 64 KB, but teachers could use the remainder as a RAM disk into which they could load all the programs and data the machine needed for class. If the machine was soft-reset the working memory would be cleared, but the data would all stay in place, ready for the next session.

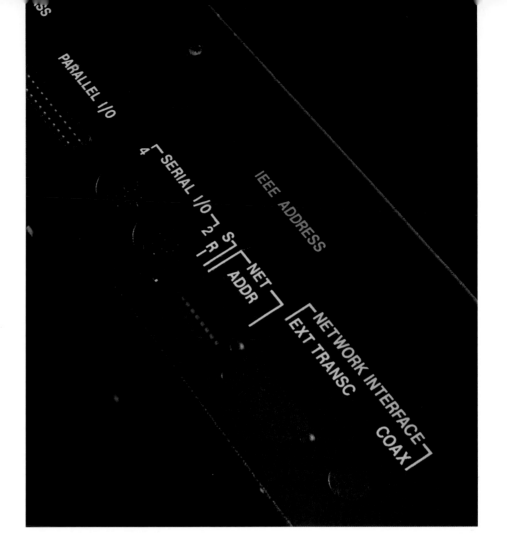

The 480Z emerged just as the British Department for Transport and Industry began a £300-million programme to promote the use of computers in schools. If half the funds were raised, the DTI would provide the second half, and the school could choose between a ZX Spectrum P. 91, a BBC Micro P. 72, and a 480Z. Over the next few years computers began to become common in schools, and in 1989 they became part of the National Curriculum. Both the 380Z and 480Z were finally discontinued in 1985, just as the DTI programme ended. They were replaced by the Intel-powered RM Nimbus series, but a generation of schoolchildren who learned the fundamentals of programming with LOGO would remember them.

MANUFACTURER
Sord Computer Corporation

AVAILABLE
1982

TECHNICAL DATA
Zilog Z80A at 4 MHz, 128 KB RAM

ORIGIN
Japan

カートリッジの損傷を防ぐ為に、カートリッジ
電源が入ったままで、
を抜きさしないでください。

PRECAUTION
TO AVOID DAMAGING CARTRIDGE
DO NOT INSERT OR REMOVE
WHILE POWER IS ON

Japanese electronics companies were quick to follow the microcomputer revolution, from NEC's 1976 release of the TK-80 kit computer, which was inspired by MOS's KIM-1 P.34, to Sharp's MZ-80K P.63. But Sord, which was founded by Takayohi Shiina in 1970 when he was 26 years old, pioneered the field.

Shiina started out writing software for PDP minicomputers, before designing the 8008-powered SMP80/08 all the way back in 1973. It never went into commercial production, so Sord's first computer was the SMP80/x, which launched alongside the Intel 8080 microprocessor in 1974, almost concurrently with MITS's Altair P.22. The later 1977 M200 was an all-in-one that closely followed the launch of the big three – the Apple II P.31, PET P.28, and TRS-80 P.27 – in the US.

The Sord M23, which was first launched in 1982, was designed for business. Sord ensured it had the software to match, backing a powerful and future-reaching programmable spreadsheet, database, and word processor package called PIPS. The M23 only shipped with text display; in order to access graphics modes, it needed a hardware upgrade and a different version of its CP/M-based operating system. Still, games were written for it, mostly in Sord's particular flavour of CBASIC. The M23 sold well and new variants followed, including the M23P in 1983, which was the first commercial computer to feature Sony's soon-to-be-standard 3½-in. disk drive, and even the truly portable A4-sized Sord IS-11, which was equipped with a small built-in LCD screen and a microcassette for storage when it was launched in 1984. Sord was a computer maker with serious technical ambition.

SORD M23 MARK III

ORIGIN
Japan

TECHNICAL DATA
Sharp Z80A at 4 MHz, 64 KB RAM

AVAILABLE
November 1982

MANUFACTURER
Sharp Corporation

SHARP MZ-700

An evolution of the MZ-40K **P. 63**, the MZ-700 was the first Sharp computer with a colour display, and the first not to feature an integrated monitor. The base model also lacked a tape drive, although the top-level one also featured a plotter that could print in four colours.

Although it only supported character-based graphics, the MZ-700 was well supported by many of the big Japanese game developers, so versions of Hudson's *Bomberman* and Tecmo's *Donkey Gorilla* appeared on it. So too did *Pitman*, a clever and original puzzle game designed by Yutaka Isokawa when he was in his teens, and which was eventually ported to Nintendo's Game Boy as *Catrap*. The object for players was to punch each ghost out of a level of obstacles, digging through dirt, pushing blocks, and climbing ladders to avoid getting trapped. If they failed, they could rewind their actions to try a new path. Although it's probably the first game ever to feature a rewind mechanic, *Pitman* was originally inspired by playing *Lode Runner* on a friend's Apple IIc **P. 31**. Isokawa found he couldn't replicate its fluid platforming with the MZ-700's blocky character graphics, but he

did manage to bend it into riffing on *Lode Runner*'s puzzle aspect, in which the player figures out the order in which they collect each gold piece while avoiding enemies.

It took Isokawa a year and a half to complete *Pitman*. With his parents concerned about how long he was spending in front of his computer, he was only allowed to use it on Sundays, so he would write out his program on paper during the week and then have just one day to type it in and debug it. Isokawa was so happy with what he produced that he submitted it to the magazine *Oh!MZ*, where the listing of the entire program, written in Hudson's HuBASIC, appeared in the August 1985 issue for readers to type into their computers. He was paid ¥10,000 for each of the seven pages.

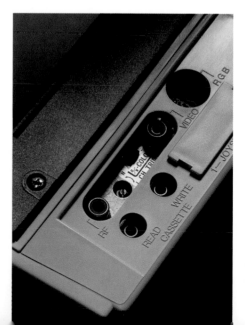

ORIGIN
Japan

TECHNICAL DATA
Zilog Z80A at 3.6 MHz, 4 KB RAM

AVAILABLE
September 1982

MANUFACTURER
Sord Computer Corporation

Alongside its more serious computers, such as the M23 P. 101, Sord also planned a low-cost computer that could take on the bottom end of the market in Japan and across the world. The Sord M5's rubber keys and cartridge slots were the kind of features that fitted the home, where it acted as a reasonable games computer, with 16 KB of its memory given to graphics, powered by a Texas Instruments TMS9918 video chip. It pushed out a 256-by-192-pixel picture with sixteen colours and support for thirty-two sprites: capabilities similar to those of the TI-99/4A P. 69 or MSX P. 133, even if it wasn't compatible with either.

The M5 could perform other roles, too: its cartridge slots gave it support for more sophisticated flavours of BASIC than the BASIC-I that shipped with it, as well as FALC, a cut-down version of PIPS, the business software that gave Sord an edge in the office. The M5 was launched in Japan in September 1982 and quickly gained a library of games and software, including titles by Konami and Namco. Outside Japan, it was launched in Korea with full language support, and in the UK in May 1983 at the rather high price of £195 by the imaginatively named Computer Games Limited, a company that specialized in importing handheld game hardware from Japan, including Konami's *Frogger* and Nintendo's *Game & Watch Donkey Kong*. Appearing at the height of the ZX Spectrum's ascendancy P. 91 and competing against all the other machines that were crowding the market, the M5 didn't gain much traction. However, as one of the first low-cost computers to appear in Czechoslovakia, it found popularity there, with users enjoying its neat implementation of BASIC.

But Sord's history was nearly over. In 1984, it began to have issues with suppliers and banks. Founder Takayohi Shiina claimed Sord was being sabotaged with an orchestrated smear campaign that declared the company was undergoing financial difficulties – all because, he said, he had a big mouth and it was making him a thorn in the side of the Japanese establishment. Despite making a tidy profit, Shiina was forced to sell Sord to Toshiba in 1985.

SORD M5

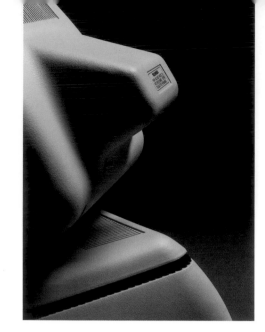

The original PET P.28 broke new ground in expanding the market for low-cost, easy-to-use microcomputers. It rapidly became the top-selling computer of its time, but there was constant opportunity for Commodore to improve it, keeping up with new technology and its expanding role in homes and offices.

First to go was the PET's awful chiclet keyboard, which was replaced in the PET's first revision in 1978 by a full-size one with a standard layout. During the following year Commodore released PETs with more memory – up to 32 KB – and upgraded ROMs. Then, in 1980, the 40 series addressed the original's small screen by increasing it to a 9-in. one, and in the same year the 80 series increased the number of characters the PET could display on each line from forty to eighty.

These constant incremental changes kept the PET up-to-date and competitive. Some changes were less technical and more about user experience. The 8032-SK exchanged the series' hitherto sharply angular design for friendly curves, and allowed its keyboard to be detached from the main computer – hence the SK ('separate keyboard') in its name – so users could have more flexibility over where the computer was positioned.

Sometimes improvements brought new problems. The one that afflicted the 40 and 80 series was the 'killer poke'. Previous PETs featured an instruction that prevented reading and writing to the video memory except during vertical blanking, the moment between the screen drawing the final line of a frame and starting to draw the first line of the next. This was to prevent snow being caused by the PET 2001's slow video chip, but because the instruction slightly slowed down text display, some programs disabled it with a POKE command. If these programs attempted to disable the instruction on the 80 series' new, faster video chip, the monitor would lose sync and the flyback transformer, which controlled its frequency, could be physically damaged. PETs might have managed to maintain compatibility as they kept up with ever-advancing technology, but that didn't mean software was always usable.

ORIGIN
United States

TECHNICAL DATA
MOS 6502 at 1 MHz, 32 KB RAM

AVAILABLE
1982

MANUFACTURER
Commodore Business Machines

COMMODORE PET 8032-SK

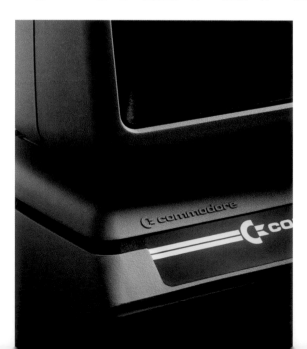

ORIGIN
United Kingdom

TECHNICAL DATA
Z80 at 4 MHz, 64 KB RAM

AVAILABLE
1983

MANUFACTURER
C/WP

In the exploding computer market of the early 1980s, the race was on for smaller manufacturers to find themselves profitable niches. The C/WP Cortex was one such attempt. Built to be a low-end office machine, it featured a Z80 microprocessor with a 6502 graphics co-processor; ran the widespread CP/M operating system; and was supplied with a monochrome screen. But it also came with various office-targeted features, such as separate dual 5.25-in. disk drives and an IBM-style keyboard designed to support command codes for a specially modified version of WordStar, which came bundled with the machine. WordStar was the dominant word processor of the time, the first to feature mail merge and WYSIWYG editing, and was so successful that in 1984 its maker, MicroPro, was the largest software company in the world. Other features addressed the Cortex's ease of maintenance and use, such as an easily removable plastic housing that boasted a dose of cheerful customization: as well as office-beige, it was also available in burnt orange and four other surprisingly bright colours.

The Cortex, which was marketed in the UK, wasn't designed by C/WP, however. It was manufactured and designed by Ontel Corporation, which was based in Georgia, US, and began marketing the machine there as the Amigo in the same year. But even the Amigo's roots don't lie in Georgia: it was originally a computer made by a company based in Asia, before Ontel bought and modified its design. Exactly which company isn't clear. Ontel's own history is lost in a fog of thirty years' worth of mergers and acquisitions, which started in 1982 when it was bought by Massachusetts-based manufacturer Visual Technology (which made yet another version of the Amigo in the form of the Visual 1050). Besides, the Cortex itself didn't do well. At £1,795 it wasn't cheap enough, and its processor was too weak. It might be largely forgotten, but it remains a symbol of the complexities of a rapidly transforming market.

C/WP CORTEX

MANUFACTURER
Camputers

AVAILABLE
September 1983

TECHNICAL DATA
Zilog Z80A at 4 MHz, 96 KB RAM

ORIGIN
United Kingdom

No matter how good its product, a new computer company faced probable ruin if it launched in the UK during 1982 or 1983. Camputers was one such example. Its only computer, the Lynx, was well designed, its restrained grey shell packed with a quick processor, a reasonable 48 KB of RAM, and high resolution 256-by-252-pixel graphics that supported eight colours. On paper, the Lynx matched or surpassed the specifications of the market-leading ZX Spectrum **P. 91** and other Z80-based systems of the time, and although it cost over twice the price of a Spectrum, it was seen as good value. But the Lynx failed. Despite releasing updated models with more RAM and higher clock speeds, such as the Lynx 96, Camputers would fold a year after it launched.

It certainly wasn't for lack of technical experience. Camputers founder Richard Greenwood began designing electronics boards in the late 1970s, subcontracting for various businesses and steadily growing a company called GWDS, which designed add-ons such as the BBC Micro's floppy drive; a full Z80-based computer, for a client who ended up shelving it; and some early work on the ill-fated NewBrain **P. 48**. Greenwood judged the team experienced enough to launch its own computer, and so work began on the Lynx in March 1982.

Perhaps the Lynx was overlooked because its graphics, although sharp for the standards of the time, were a lot slower than the other machines on the market. Perhaps Camputers didn't move to support it with software until far too late, and it certainly had far too few games. Ultimately, the Lynx was marked out as a programmer's machine; its implementation of BASIC included various neat features, such as automatic indenting and efficient commands such as REPEAT/UNTIL, and its ROM featured a machine code editor. Perhaps it took too long to ship; the first (48-KB) Lynx was meant to launch in October 1982, but, following issues with bugs in its BASIC and with its motherboard, it wasn't available in shops until the following March. But the biggest reason for its failure was simply the time in which the Lynx was born.

CAMPUTERS LYNX 96

ORIGIN
United States

TECHNICAL DATA
Zilog Z80 at 4 MHz and Intel 8088
at 4.81 MHz, 64 KB RAM

AVAILABLE
June 1982

MANUFACTURER
Digital Equipment Corporation

With two processors – a 16-bit Intel 8088 and an 8-bit Zilog Z80 – and the ability to boot into both MS-DOS and CP/M, the Rainbow should have been the single machine you needed to handle a huge swathe of all the software released for the multifarious competing processors and operating systems of the early 1980s. The Rainbow may sound like it was over-engineered, but both processors were used for general functions as well as programs; the Z80 controlled the Rainbow's storage drives, while the 8088 controlled video, keyboard, and printer. But this powerful machine came too late to stand up to the new leader in office computing.

The Rainbow was made by Digital Equipment Corporation (DEC), a company that was second in size only to IBM during the early 1980s. It was the creator of the groundbreaking PDP series of minicomputers, which were common across businesses and universities, but the microcomputer had began to grow as a practical low-cost alternative to the room-filling machines that DEC made. Especially after 1981, when IBM launched its own bid for the microcomputer market in the form of the 5150 P. 66, DEC realized it was time to join in.

Unfortunately for DEC, the Rainbow didn't make its mark. The IBM PC wasn't nearly as generalist as the Rainbow, but backed by IBM's might, it very quickly defined a standard for professional computing. And although the Rainbow supported MS-DOS, its hardware was different enough to prevent it from being fully compatible with IBM's personal computer, while CP/M programs had to be re-compiled for the Rainbow. It took long months before leading office software such as Lotus 1-2-3 was available for it in native form, and it didn't help that its proprietary and rather eccentric RX50 floppy drive meant buying expensive disks from DEC. As CP/M began to lose ground to DOS, the Rainbow looked increasingly backward, unable even to support the large library of software developed for DEC's PDP systems. Still, DEC released various versions of the Rainbow, from the floppy-drive-based 100 to the 100+, at $5,475, which came with a pre-installed Winchester hard drive of up to 67 MB.

DEC RAINBOW

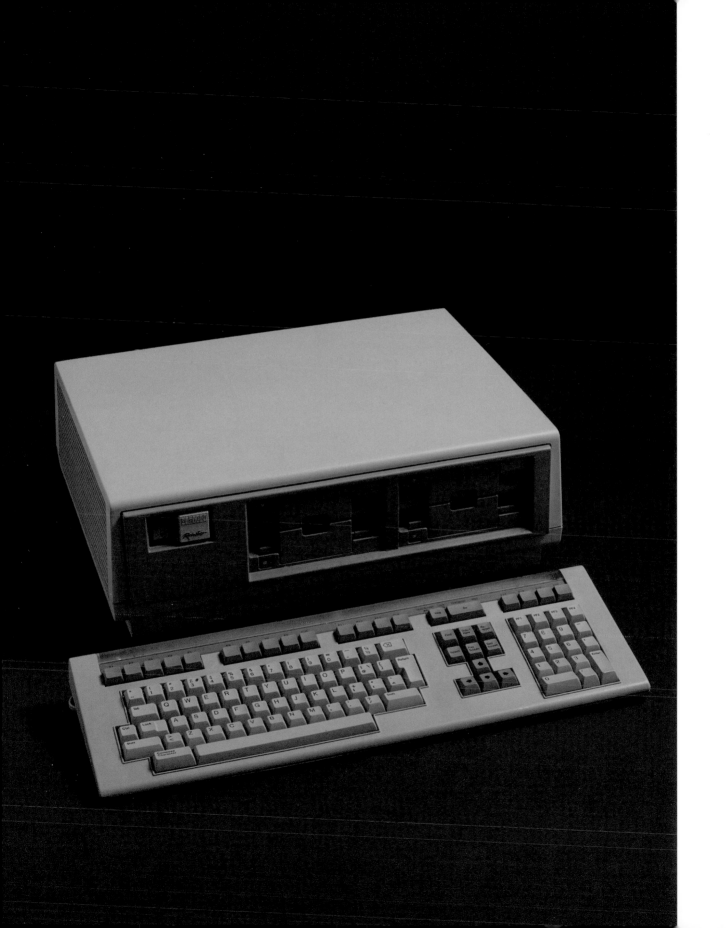

ORIGIN
Federal Republic of Germany (FRG)

TECHNICAL DATA
Intel 8086, 128 KB RAM

AVAILABLE
1983

MANUFACTURER
Olympia International

The Olympia People wanted to be whatever every office user wanted it to be. Although it wasn't strictly IBM-compatible, it came with a version of MS-DOS 2.0, and it was also supplied with CP/M-86 Plus, which supported the multitasking operating system Concurrent DOS 3.1. Also developed by Research Machines, Concurrent DOS could run up to four applications at once, although it only had basic compatibility with DOS, and couldn't run screen-dependent applications such as Wordstar. The People was also supplied with GSX-86, Digital Research's graphical extension for CP/M and a precursor to GEM, its graphical user interface. All in all, the People covered all the key business operating systems and functions of its era.

It was also clearly robust and reliable, with a wonderfully chunky keyboard built by Japanese manufacturer Fujitsu. Olympia prided itself on the People's sturdy construction, with casing made from metal rather than plastic, a choice that was perhaps a legacy of Olympia's heritage as a typewriter manufacturer. Founded in Germany in 1903, Olympia Werke was one of the three biggest office equipment manufacturers in the world by 1970 – novelist Paul Auster has one of their typewriters, and even wrote a book about it.

From 1970, however, Olympia's fortunes had begun to falter. It had come from an industry in which products were built to last, but the computer industry was very different; obsolescence was built into every machine. It had been slow to shift to making computers, and it was quickly left behind by younger and nimbler companies. In 1991 it closed down its office business with the loss of over 3,600 jobs. Its US subsidiary continued to market nondescript PCs into the 1990s, but Olympia had long stopped being the giant it used to be.

OLYMPIA PEOPLE

MANUFACTURER
Applied Computer Techniques

AVAILABLE
September 1983

TECHNICAL DATA
Intel 8086 at 4.77 MHz, 256 KB RAM

ORIGIN
United Kingdom

Apricot was founded as Applied Computer Techniques (ACT) in 1965, and in the 1980s it became one of the UK's premier computer manufacturers with a series of technically advanced machines aimed squarely at professionals. Many of its computers were pioneering, including the 16-bit Apricot PC, which was the first all-in-one computer fitted with Sony's new 3½-in. disk drive and supported a then-stunning graphics resolution of 800 by 400 pixels.

The Apricot PC was based on a computer called the Sirius 1, which ACT had great success distributing from 1982. A rebadged Victor 9000, originated by 6502 designer Chuck Peddle, the Sirius 1 featured the same resolution as the Apricot PC. It became the most popular 16-bit computer in Europe, despite a UK price of over £2,500, because it featured many of the technical strengths of the IBM PC P.66 before it was officially released there.

The Apricot PC was designed in ACT's research and development centre in Birmingham, England, and built at its factory in Glenrothes, near Edinburgh, Scotland, and it was intended to maintain the momentum started by the Sirius 1. Almost every aspect of the Apricot PC was advanced in some way, from the low profile of its sparingly designed casing right down to its MicroKey keyboard, which featured an LCD screen that displayed the function of its six programmable keys.

Like the Sirius 1, it also ran both the MS-DOS and CP/M operating systems, and it was incompatible with IBM's PC standard. That was a decision that served the Apricot fine at the time, since IBM PCs took so long to get into Europe, but ACT should have noticed that the Victor 9000 didn't do well in the US, where it failed to compete against IBM's might. Once the IBM PC was finally released in Europe, ACT began to feel the same pressure, but rather than bending to the new PC standard, it responded by doubling down on powerful and innovative computers, from 1984's Apricot Portable, which featured an eighty-character, twenty-five-line LCD display and voice command recognition, to the XEN-I, which was marketed as being cheaper and more powerful than the IBM AT. And so ACT continued to grow, entirely insulated from the war raging among cheap home computers, and in spite of IBM's dominance over the PC.

APRICOT PC

Apricot PC, keyboard, detail ↑

ORIGIN
UK

TECHNICAL DATA
Intel 8086 at 4.6 MHz, 128 KB RAM

AVAILABLE
1983

MANUFACTURER
Micro Networks

Samurai was a strong name for a business computer in the 1980s, implying power and thrusting effectiveness, along with a formal kind of efficiency and decorum. So it's natural that there was some competition for the right to use it in the UK of the early 1980s.

The Samurai S16 was the winner, even though it was an otherwise reasonably nondescript 8086-based business computer, very similar to the Olympia People, right down to its support for Concurrent CP/M P. 114, and the Apricot PC P. 117. It was powerful, expandable, and expensive at over £3,000, and it made almost no impact on the history of the home computer – except through its name.

The S16's competitor for the name 'Samurai' was a UK-based computer maker called Enterprise, which was struggling to find a name to give to a rather more ambitious computer that wouldn't appear on the market for quite a long time yet P. 175. But Micro Networks had managed to grab the name by issuing an advertisement in early 1983 that stated, 'the Samurai home computer is coming', without detailing when or what it would actually be. Enterprise attempted to challenge Micro Networks for 'Samurai' but was told it was trademarked, and so its search for a name continued.

The Samurai S16 was not designed in the UK. Instead, it was a rebadged KDS 7861, made by Tokyo-based company Kokusai Electric Co. Founded in 1949, the company was a pioneer in microwave ovens and radio broadcasting technology, and operated in many other electronics industries besides. Micro Networks traded on the computer's Japanese heritage, its advertisements celebrating it emerging from 'the world's most powerful economy', lending it a price that gave it 'a decisive edge over the competition from the other side of the Pacific'. But the Samurai was already behind the curve, as that other side of the Pacific was already turning towards the new hardware standard set by IBM.

MICRO NETWORKS
SAMURAI S16

COMPAQ
PORTABLE

ORIGIN
United States

TECHNICAL DATA
Intel 8088 at 4.77 MHz, 128 KB–640 KB
RAM

AVAILABLE
March 1983

MANUFACTURER
Compaq

When IBM designed the 5150 P. 66, it unwittingly opened the way for the end of its rule over the PC's future. The 5150's components were standardized and available to buy; its architecture was open, so anyone could design hardware and software for it; and it used Microsoft's DOS as its operating system. The one thing that actually made the IBM PC *IBM's* was its patented BIOS.

The BIOS was firmware that the IBM PC used to boot up, get DOS running, and provide it with access to devices such as its keyboard and display. If someone could 'clean-room' IBM's 8-KB BIOS, building a new one that could perform the exact same functions but was not based on any knowledge of how IBM's BIOS worked, they could legally ship their own PC, compatible with the hundreds of software packages and hardware peripherals that had been created for IBM's. It could even include DOS, since Microsoft had retained the right to license it to other companies.

The first to succeed was Columbia Data Products, which launched the MPC 1600 in June 1982. For the same specifications, an MPC cost $3,395 and an IBM PC cost around $7,000. The MPC sold well, but being fundamentally the same machine, it was exposed to competition with all the clones that were to follow.

The second company to clone IBM's BIOS didn't follow its source's lead. The Compaq Portable, which was announced in November 1982, just over a year after the 5150 entered the market, was not desk-bound. It packed its 9-in. monochrome CRT screen, keyboard, and all into a suitcase-like casing complete with carrying handle. At over 12 kg (26½ lb), it wasn't exactly light, and it had no on-board battery, but it was specifically designed to fit in aeroplane overhead bins and therefore appealed to a class of business people for whom the computer was becoming increasingly indispensable. Thus, though more expensive than other IBM-compatibles, the Portable was an immediate success, selling 53,000 units in its first year. It hastened the rise not only of the PC era, but also of the portable one.

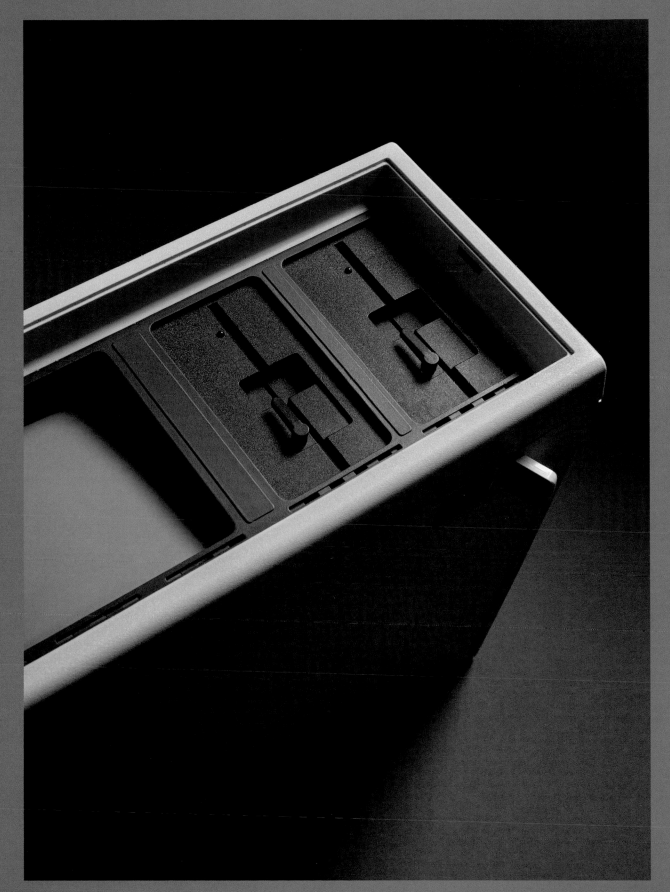

Compaq Portable, keyboard attachment (closed) ↓

Compaq Portable, keyboard attachment (open) ↓

ORIGIN
United States

TECHNICAL DATA
Zilog Z80 at 3.25 MHz, 16 KB RAM

AVAILABLE
July 1983

MANUFACTURER
Timex Sinclair

It was a profound shock to the market. In July 1982, when the Timex Sinclair 1000 launched in the US, it was the first computer to be sold for under $100 and propelled a developing price war into direct conflict. By its end, the war caused Texas Instruments to be knocked out of the home computer industry. Not bad for a ZX81 repurposed to support US NTSC-format TVs and fitted with extra RAM.

Timex Corporation, which was originally founded as a clock maker in Connecticut in the mid-19th century, had a hard time facing the electronic revolution of the 1970s. Digital watches seemed to be making its mechanical watches obsolete, so Timex got into electronics, and its factory in Dundee, Scotland, built computers including the ZX81 and Spectrum P.91 for Sinclair. Before long, the two companies decided to launch a joint venture to release Sinclair's machines in the US, the first being the 1000 in July 1982.

Half a million 1000s sold within six months, and at one point Timex Sinclair claimed 28 per cent of the US home computer market. Commodore, with its entry-level VIC-20 P.56, and Texas Instruments, with its TI-99/4A P.69, saw that they needed to further cut their prices to compete. Soon the war pulled in higher-end computers; Commodore offered $100 towards the price of a Commodore 64 P.79 if a customer traded in a competing computer. Since the TS 1000 had been reduced to just $50, many customers bought one simply to get the larger discount on a rather better machine.

A year later, Timex Sinclair launched an upgraded 1000 in the form of the 1500. It featured 16 KB of RAM and a classic Sinclair rubber keyboard instead of the 1000's touch-sensitive one, but it was still the same limited machine, and because it retailed at $79.95 it immediately struggled against Commodore's ability to undercut prices and oversupply the market. Timex Sinclair's last computer in the US, the Spectrum-based 2068, launched in November 1983, but it wasn't enough: the company pulled out of the whole endeavour in early 1984, calling the home computer market 'risky and volatile'. It was a situation much of its own making.

TIMEX SINCLAIR 1500

MANUFACTURER
Mattel Electronics

AVAILABLE
June 1983

TECHNICAL DATA
NEC Z80A at 3.5 MHz, 4 KB RAM

ORIGIN
United States

It was one of the most short-lived computers ever made. The Mattel Aquarius lasted just four months on the market before it was pulled, the victim of dated hardware design. The toy giant never made a computer again.

Before the release of the Aquarius, Mattel had already carved itself a leading position in the world of computers with the release of the Intellivision gaming console in 1980. It had always intended to release a keyboard-based expansion that would turn the Intellivision into a full computer, but following various issues with build costs and reliability this never came to fruition, causing Mattel, which had advertised it as a feature, to be fined by the Federal Trade Commission for false advertising. In its place came the hurriedly developed BASIC-based Entertainment Computer System add-on, which launched with little real commitment in 1983. By then, the home computer revolution was in full flood and the ECS looked hopelessly backward – and Mattel was already about to release a standalone computer.

Mattel didn't design the Aquarius itself, instead approaching third parties and settling on Hong Kong-based Radofin, which was founded in the mid-1970s and manufactured calculators, TV games, and hardware, including the Intellivision, under contract. It just happened that Radofin already had a Z80-powered design ready to go: Mattel announced it in 1982 and showed it for the first time in January 1983, before releasing it in June.

The world was unimpressed. With just 4 KB of RAM, one-voice sound, no sprite support, no programmable characters for graphics, and no game controllers, it was hopelessly outclassed by the incumbent home computers on the market. Mattel reacted, adding an expanded character set that included more graphics options and a series of memory expansion cartridges, alongside various expansions. It even planned two successors, the Aquarius II and III. But sales were so low that the Aquarius was discontinued in October 1983, ending Mattel's attempt to be a computer maker. It wasn't the end of the Aquarius, however. In January 1984, Radofin took all unsold stock and for the next two years manufactured more, distributing it under new names.

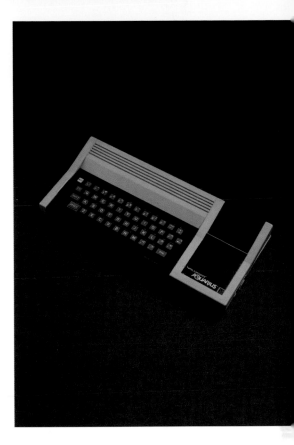

MATTEL AQUARIUS

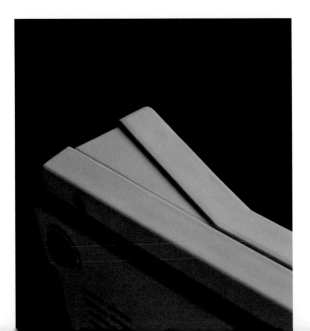

ORIGIN
United States

TECHNICAL DATA
MOS 6502C at 1.8 MHz, 16 KB RAM

AVAILABLE
October 1983

MANUFACTURER
Atari Inc.

ATARI 600XL

Although Atari's 400 and 800 P.40 got a lot right, they entered a world dominated by the PET P.26, VIC-20 P.56, Apple II P.31, and TRS-80 P.27, and Atari found competition hard. To turn a profit, it had to reduce costs, and so in 1983 it launched the first in a new series of computers that used the 400 and 800 as its base. The 1200XL was designed to be less expensive to build, omitting an expansion connector and some other details, but it had 64 KB of RAM. At $899, it was immediately criticized as being too expensive: so expensive, rumours claimed, that it caused sales of the much cheaper 800 to go up during the few short months the 1200XL was on sale.

In fact, it was more likely that the 800's sales went up because Atari slashed its price to $165 in mid-1983 to keep up with the price war that began with a scuffle between the TI-99/4A P.69 and VIC-20 and soon embroiled every home computer. Atari's response was announced in the summer of 1983: successors to the 400 and 800, the 600XL and 800XL. They were both designed along the same lines as the 1200XL, sharing its two-tone chassis and full keyboard, but were slimmer, and although the 600XL only shipped with 16 KB of RAM, the 800XL had 64 KB and a new ANTIC video controller that added extra graphics modes.

The 800XL went on to become Atari's top-selling computer, but Atari was in trouble. In September 1983 it dumped into a landfill in New Mexico fourteen truckloads of computer parts and game cartridges, many rumoured to have been for its much-mocked 2600 game, *E.T. the Extra-Terrestrial*. Over the course of 1983, Atari lost $536 million, largely as a result of falling game sales: the legendary videogame crash. In the following July, parent company Warner Communications sold the company, putting its fortunes into the hands of someone who had previously been its cutthroat competitor P.186.

ORIGIN
United States

TECHNICAL DATA
Zilog Z80A at 3.6 MHz, 48 KB RAM

AVAILABLE
June 1983

MANUFACTURER
Spectravideo

The first piece of hardware that Harry Fox and Alex Weiss released was the Quickshot, a novel joystick that was ergonomically shaped to the player's hand. The next would end up setting an entire hardware standard.

Their company, Spectravideo, then known as Spectravision, started out distributing games for the Atari 2600, ColecoVision, and VIC-20 P. 56, but Fox and Weiss saw a future in making a computer. Working with a Hong Kong-based electronics manufacturer called Bondwell, they came up with a design based on the Z80 microprocessor; Texas Instruments' TMS9918 video processor; General Instrument's AY-3-8910 sound chip; and 16 KB of RAM. They called it the SVI-318, and first revealed it at Consumer Electronics Show in January 1983.

But they needed to license a version of BASIC and, having failed to make contact with Microsoft in the US, they eventually met Kazuhiko Nishi, founder of Japanese publishing and software house ASCII and head of Microsoft Japan. He saw that the SVI-318's design was both cheap to manufacture and flexible, and he also saw in it the potential to meet his plans to set a standard PC specification that he would go on to call the MSX P. 133. But he wanted to make some changes, making it more easily expandable so it would last on the market for longer.

The truth is, the SVI-318 wasn't actually compatible with the MSX format. It ran Microsoft Extended BASIC, not MSX BASIC, and its BIOS, disk format, and interface ports were all slightly different. While Spectravideo readied the 318 for launch, Nishi rallied most major Japanese manufacturers around the MSX standard – but Fox didn't feel able to effectively negotiate worldwide terms for them all, especially since the final 318 was in fact heavily adapted by Nishi. So he offered Nishi a deal: Nishi could design his own version if he could make it just different enough that he didn't have to license it from Spectravideo.

And so Nishi formulated the MSX and Spectravideo went its own way, and into obscurity. Not being true MSX machines, the 318 and higher-end 328 sold badly, and Spectravideo sold its stock to Bondwell in 1984. In 1985 Bondwell finally released a truly MSX-compatible machine, the SVI-728.

SPECTRAVIDEO SVI-328 MK II

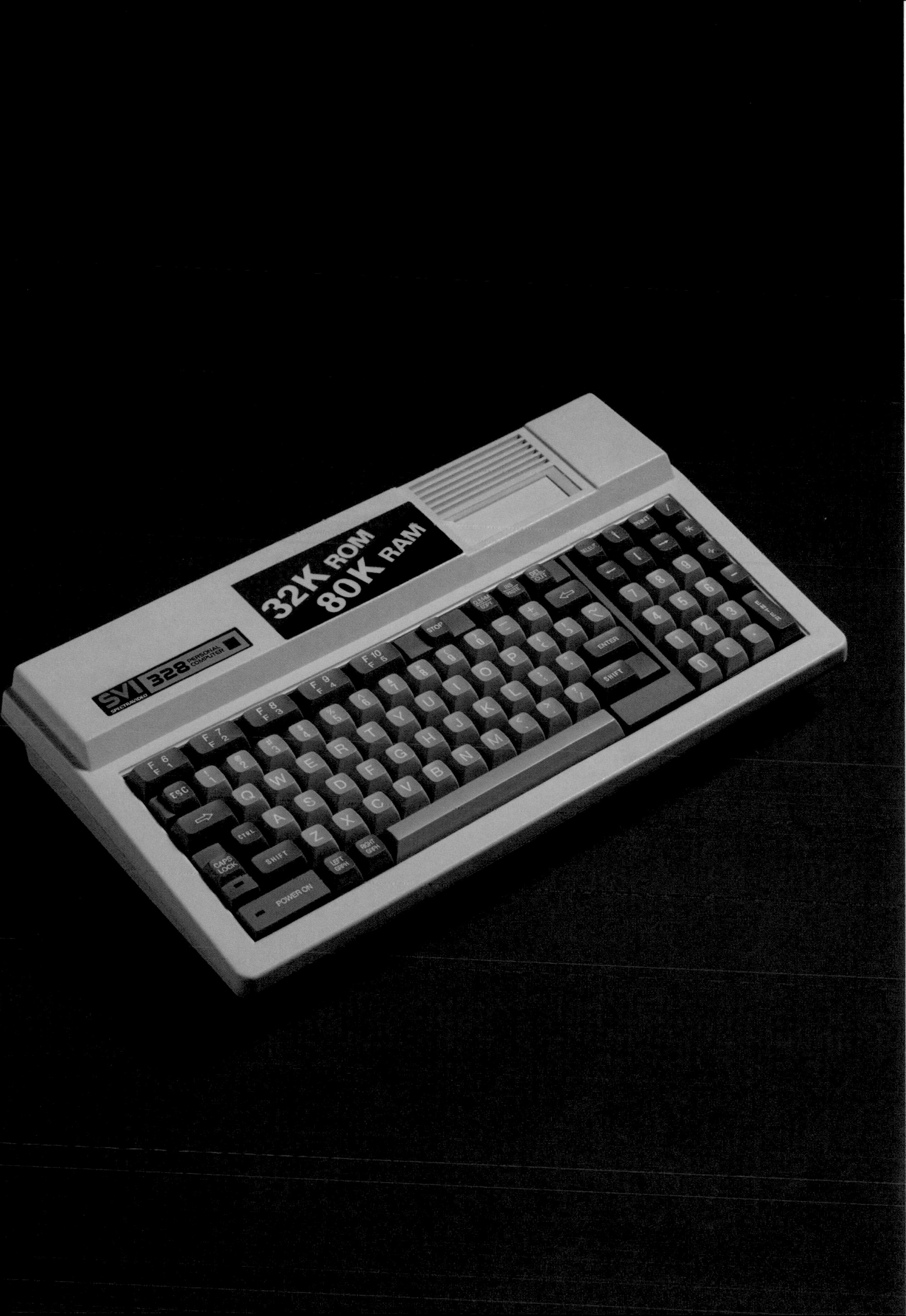

Detail, Spectravideo SVI-328 MK II ↑

TOSHIBA HX-10

ORIGIN
Japan

TECHNICAL DATA
Zilog Z80A at 3.6 MHz, 64 KB RAM

AVAILABLE
June 1983

MANUFACTURER
Toshiba Corporation

When Kazuhiko Nishi dropped out of university in 1976 to help found *I/O*, the first computing magazine, he began a career as a central part of the Japanese computer industry. The NEC TK-80 kit had just launched, and Japanese hobbyists were flocking to build computers for themselves – but when he visited San Francisco in April 1977, Nishi realized that Japan was behind. The 'personal computer revolution', as he put it, had begun with the launches of the Apple II **P. 31**, PET **P. 28**, and TRS-80 **P. 27**. The next month he founded ASCII Publishing Corporation with Keiichiro Tsukamoto, publishing *ASCII* magazine for the computer business and *I/O* for users. ASCII would soon grow outside magazines and into software publishing, particularly games, and it also led to Nishi meeting Microsoft cofounder Bill Gates. The two hit it off immediately (Nishi claims that he talked Gates into putting MS-DOS forward for the IBM PC **P. 66**), and ASCII became Microsoft's agent in Japan.

All the while, Nishi also had a hand in hardware. He helped develop NEC's groundbreaking 1979 PC-8001, but he had a bigger hand in bringing about the MSX. Nishi saw the computer landscape of the early 1980s as a forest of competing platforms and incompatible variants of BASIC. MSX was an attempt to establish a standardized format, built with off-the-shelf components. Based on the Spectravideo SV-328 **P. 130**, it featured a Z80 microprocessor, a Texas Instruments TMS9918 graphics chip and a General Instrument AY-3-8910 sound and I/O chip, and it was bound together by Microsoft's MSX BASIC.

It has been estimated that over five million MSX systems were sold in Japan across four generations and over seven years, and the system served as the origin of hit game series such as *Metal Gear* and *Bomberman*. But it didn't have the same impact outside Japan; Toshiba's MSX-format HX-10 was released in Europe, but only in 1984, when it was forced to compete against the might of the Commodore 64, Spectrum, and other incumbents.

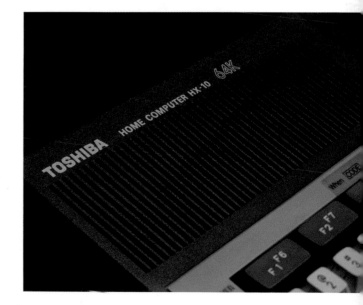

MANUFACTURER
Canon

AVAILABLE
June 1984

TECHNICAL DATA
NEC 280A at 3.6 MHz, 64 KB RAM

ORIGIN
Japan

Canon's entry for the MSX format was the V-10, which came in a neat white casing but was limited by its 16 KB of RAM. Though the first MSX specification allowed just 8 KB of RAM, it was soon apparent that it needed more to fully realize the format's potential. So the following year Canon released the V-20, which had 64 KB of RAM and a black case, and it became a strong part of the MSX's initial wave: enough to see it being exported to sell in the UK and France from 1985.

Canon was better known for its imaging technology – cameras, printers, and photocopiers – but it wasn't new to building computers when it released the V-10 and V-20. Its first were the AX-1 in 1978, which incorporated a calculator-like algebraic programming language and a small display, and then the AS-100, a 16-bit business computer, in 1982. Its MSX computers were, however, its first forays into the world of games and home use.

But Canon had always had an interest in exploring ways in which computers could be integrated with cameras. After all, in 1976 it was the first manufacturer to fit a microcomputer in a camera with the AE-1. The V-20, along with the other MSX computers of its generation, could be connected via its cartridge slot to a Canon T-90 camera fitted with the Data Memory Back 90, in order to display or print out exposure data, save it to tape, and set text that could be imprinted into photographs. It was a very early example of a home computer becoming part of a multimedia toolkit.

CANON V-20

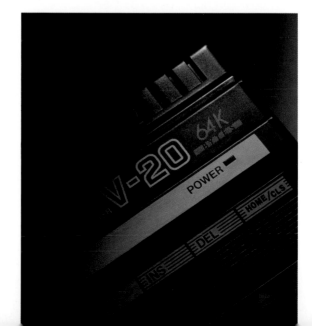

ORIGIN
France

TECHNICAL DATA
Motorola 6803 at 0.89 MHz, 4 KB RAM

AVAILABLE
Autumn 1983

MANUFACTURER
Matra Hachette

Jean-Luc Lagardère, CEO of Matra, had an ambition. He wanted to enable the French people to 'follow the microcomputer revolution without any complexities'. For him, that meant making a simple computer that was accompanied by an easy-to-follow French-language manual. In that context, the Matra Alice's toy-like appearance, with its deep red casing, friendly logo, and small size, made a lot of sense, even if it was produced by a company that specialized in aircraft engines.

Underneath its casing, however, the Matra Alice was a TRS-80 MC-10, licensed to Matra by Tandy and built in the Alsace. In the US the MC-10 was a failure, a cut-down computer designed to compete with the Timex Sinclair P. 124. Its chiclet keyboard, 4 KB of RAM (which left only 3 KB for programs), and aged, somewhat obscure 6803 processor were decidedly backward for the time and lacked software. And yet the Alice cost 1,200 francs, the equivalent of about £115 at the time and around the same price as the rather more practically attractive ZX Spectrum P. 91.

Matra was not the only company behind the Alice. It was a collaboration with the publishing corporation Hachette, which produced a manual that was praised for its accessible tone, even if it didn't go into much detail on such arcane matters as machine code. The manual's cover, along with the Alice's box, was illustrated by comic artist Moebius, who depicted the machine levitating in front of a cross-legged and apparently meditating girl, like a piece of the fantasy future technology he would normally draw but alongside the everyday paraphernalia – books, pillows, snacks – of a modern young life. The Alice looked surprisingly natural hovering there, but that was probably because Moebius didn't show the trailing wires needed to connect it to a power output and a TV. It might not have been a marvel by any other metric, but the Alice was, alongside Sinclair's work, an early example of how design and art could elevate and communicate something greater about a mundane slab of silicon and plastic.

MATRA ALICE

ORIGIN
Hong Kong

TECHNICAL DATA
Zilog Z80A at 3.58 MHz, 4 KB RAM

AVAILABLE
November 1983

MANUFACTURER
Video Technology

VTECH LASER 200

As leaders began to emerge in the home computer revolution, fringe companies sprang forward to build clones. Many computers were built from standardized parts, so if they could use the components and architectures of the most popular machines, companies such as Dragon **P. 95** and Matra **P. 136** could release their own versions, able to run the same software and appeal to the same buyers, competing through compatibility.

Video Technology, now known as VTech, was founded in Hong Kong in 1976 to develop TV and handheld games, but its first computer was the 1982 Laser 100. It was fundamentally identical to the TRS-80 **P. 27**, and the BASIC that ran on it was altered – by removing some routines and adding a different line editor – just enough to allow VTech to avoid being sued for copyright. With a cheap keyboard and light plastic case, VTech could undercut Tandy's price.

The colour Laser 200 took on the TRS-80 Color Computer **P. 53**, using the same video chip, but because it retained the 100's Z80-powered main board, it wasn't actually compatible with the CoCo. Its function-emblazoned keyboard, meanwhile, seemed to invoke Sinclair's computers. The Laser 200 was sold worldwide under various different badges, such as the Dick Smith VZ 200 in Australasia (alongside the Genie series); the Salora Fellow in Finland; and the Smart-Alec Jr. in the US. In the UK it was known as

the Texet TX-8000. At under £100, it was the cheapest colour computer on the market, costing less than the ZX Spectrum P.91 and Oric-1 P.97, but it made little headway against them.

Video Technology went on to produce more generations of the Laser series, including the 128, which was a clone of the Apple IIe P.31. Its ROM was the product of clean-room design: in a move similar to the way in which Compaq reproduced the IBM 5150's BIOS P.120, Video Technology reproduced the Apple II's core software without looking at it and therefore without risking being accused of breaching its copyright. Apple failed to file a lawsuit to stop it from being distributed, so the company continued to build computers and further diversify, and remains in operation today.

ACORN ELECTRON

ORIGIN
United Kingdom

TECHNICAL DATA
MOS Technology 6502A at 2 MHz when accessing ROM or 1 MHz/0.5897 MHz when accessing RAM, 32 KB RAM

AVAILABLE
August 1983

MANUFACTURER
Acorn Computers

The ZX Spectrum's **P.91** £175 launch price immediately undercut the 16-KB Acorn BBC Micro Model A's £235 **P.72**. Acorn may have won the BBC's contract, but cofounder Hermann Hauser knew that price would transcend even the national promotion the BBC Micro was enjoying, and a couple of months later he told *Popular Computing Weekly* that a cheaper Acorn was in the works.

The idea was to create a chopped-down BBC Micro that would be extensible so it could keep up with its big brother. It would use an uncommitted logic array (ULA), a single general-purpose chip that could be configured to perform the role of lots of separate chips without Acorn having to design a chip from scratch: the very same technique that made the ZX81 cheaper than the ZX80 **P.74**. Technical lead Steve Furber squeezed the 100-odd chips inside the BBC Micro down to just over ten – but the ULA would end up harming the Electron.

It didn't help that the ULA could only output one channel of sound compared to the BBC Micro's four. It lacked the BBC Micro's memory-cheap teletext video mode, causing AcornSoft to have to re-write many programs to support it, and the processor had to work at half the speed when running programs stored in RAM. Furber *also* noticed pixels flickering when the Electron was set to its graphics mode. ULA maker Ferranti thought this was caused by Furber's design, while Furber figured it was the silicon. It turned out to be down to electromagnetic noise made by the voltage regulator, but fixing it took time.

The Electron was finally launched a year after Hauser first mentioned it, costing £199 rather than the £150 Acorn had been promising. The Spectrum had been discounted to £130. Acorn still boasted of 150,000 orders for the Electron in October 1983, but problems continued. Acorn couldn't make them fast enough, with some blaming Ferranti for only being able to manufacture one working ULA in ten. It was several months before the Electron was being made in the numbers Acorn planned: just in time for the end of the computer boom in 1984. Acorn ended up stuck with stock worth £43 million. Difficult times lay ahead **P.211**.

MANUFACTURER
Memotech Computers

AVAILABLE
1983

TECHNICAL DATA
Zilog Z80A at 4 MHz, 64 KB RAM

ORIGIN
United Kingdom

MTX512

MEMOTECH
MTX512

Around the home computers of the early 1980s grew a cottage industry of peripheral makers, who looked for opportunities to sell specialized devices that overcame hardware deficiencies and added new functions. Many were cheaply made and unreliable, but some, such as Memotech's Memopak RAM add-ons for the ZX81 P.71, were fantastic pieces of engineering, smartly designed and presented in quality metal cases.

While it made good money producing Memopaks, Memotech also developed a video-digitizing system called HRX that called for a powerful custom Z80B-based computer called the SM1. The SM1 never went on sale, but when the ZX Spectrum's more fulsome specification P.91 began to eat away at the memory add-on business, Memotech decided to refashion the SM1 into a cheaper machine that would compete with the BBC Micro P.72 while also offering expansion interfaces that might suit business and educational uses. The result was a finely engineered and powerful computer with dedicated video RAM and a full keyboard, all inside a black brushed-aluminium case.

Its software was also accomplished. MTX Basic came with the ability to edit the last twenty-four lines of a program, and then checked its syntax (although its error messages didn't give an awful lot of information on what was actually wrong). Its shortcuts enabled users to type a single letter for commands; for example, if the user typed 'P' followed by a full stop, the computer would fill in the full PRINT command.

But the MTX500 and 512 (with 32 KB and 64 KB of RAM respectively) were high-end home computers that emerged into a saturated market. Sales were low, despite price cuts that saw the 512 falling from £315 to £130 at the end of 1985, and Memotech folded in 1986 after launching a follow-up, the RS128. But they found an afterlife. Cofounder Geoff Boyd bought the company's assets, cannily seeing an opportunity to pivot away from the home computer and towards using MTX machines to control video walls: banks of TVs configured to display a single large image. There they had great success, providing the 'Quadrascope' wall for the Natural History Museum in London and many others.

ORIGIN
Netherlands

TECHNICAL DATA
2 x Zilog Z80A at 4 MHz, 64 KB RAM

AVAILABLE
1983

MANUFACTURER
Philips

If the Compaq Portable **P. 120** and Commodore SX-64 **P. 165** weren't heavy enough, here's the Philips P2000C. It weighed 15 kg (33 lb), putting it on the very edge of the concept of 'luggable'. But, fitted with a 9-in. green-screen monitor, two floppy drives, and a wide choice of expansion interfaces – including up to seven hard drives – it was a capable and flexible machine.

The P2000 range was Philips' gambit for making computers aimed at homes and small businesses, having dabbled in the late 1970s with a game console system that was best known as the Magnavox Odyssey[2]. The range started in 1980 with the Z80-powered P2000T, which ended up being heavily used in Dutch schools and among hobbyists – although it was expensive and only supported teletext modes, so it couldn't support games and thus attract broader appeal.

More versions followed, up to the P2000C, which was a more serious bid for business use, although none of the versions was compatible with the others. The P2000C's use of CP/M gave it access to typical business software such as Wordstar. More powerfully, though, it could run MS-DOS when fitted with Philips' own 8088 Copower board, which contained an 8088 processor and up to 512 KB of additional RAM, and came with a copy of MS-DOS version 2.11. Expansion boards such as this enabled Z80-based systems to run some IBM-compatible software. The P2000C Copower board struggled to support 'badly behaved' software that used unauthorized features of the IBM BIOS, but it featured two compatibility modes for 'well-behaved' and 'poorly behaved' software, as the manual called it. It was complex to use, but added even more adaptability for this heavyweight portable.

PHILIPS P2OOOC

APPLE LISA 2

ORIGIN
United States

TECHNICAL DATA
Motorola MC68000 at 5 MHz, 1 MB RAM

AVAILABLE
January 1984

MANUFACTURER
Apple Computer

Until the Lisa, home computers were a blinking cursor on a black background. In order to interact with them, you had to type in arcane commands with syntaxes that usually varied between machines and languages. Furthermore, programs invariably imposed their own ways of working, with their own conventions of control and proprietary data formats.

The Lisa introduced a new way to interact with computers. It was the first home microcomputer to feature a graphical user interface, or GUI: a way of presenting the abstractions of a computer's workings through visual metaphors. Data was arranged as folders and pads of paper and displayed as icons on a desktop and in a series of windows. The calculator looked like the real thing, with buttons you could click on to input numbers, and menus of commands pulled down from the top of the screen. It featured a clipboard that could copy and cut data from one program and paste it into another. And it used a pointing device – a mouse – to select and control it all.

None of these ideas was strictly new. Lisa OS, the Lisa's operating system, was heavily influenced by the remarkable research that was performed at Xerox PARC during the 1970s, the first commercial expression of which was the 1981 Xerox Star workstation. But the Lisa was still the result of $50 million worth of Apple's own research and development, and through that, Apple became the first company to introduce to the wider public a more friendly, more human-based way of working with computers.

Well, the most wealthy slice of the public, anyway. The Lisa cost $9,995 at its launch in January 1983, a figure that was necessary to cover its cavernous 1 MB of RAM, high-resolution screen, and other non-standard features. It was not a success. Still, Apple kept at the Lisa, releasing, a year later, the Lisa 2, which had half the RAM and a Sony 3½-in. disk drive so that it could start at a far more reasonable $3,495. But the Macintosh P. 151 was only months away from entirely taking the wind from the Lisa's sails.

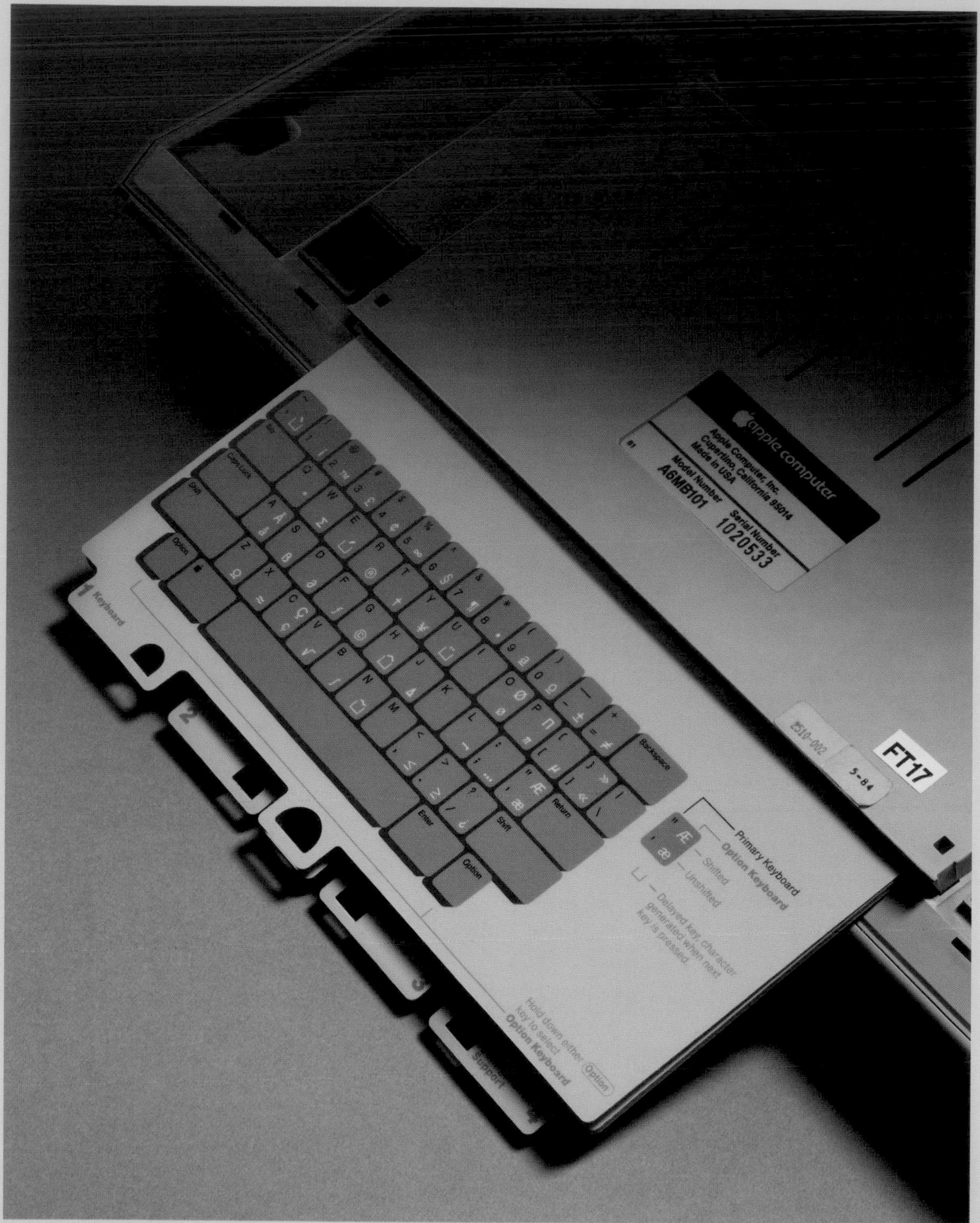

Apple Lisa 2, pull-out information cards ↓

ORIGIN
United States

TECHNICAL DATA
Motorola 68000 at 7.8 MHz, 128 KB RAM

AVAILABLE
January 1984

MANUFACTURER
Apple Computer

APPLE
MACINTOSH

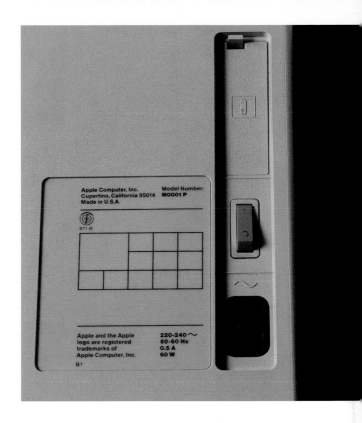

The Macintosh's legacy is such that it nearly lived up to the bombast of its legendary '1984' Super Bowl TV advert. In fact, its development and launch was a lot more shaky: a story of corporate politics from both within and outside Apple.

Its roots were in a project that began in 1979 and aimed to build a low-cost multitasking computer. Initially designed with a restrained specification, it was developed alongside the Lisa P. 146, and it wasn't long before the team incorporated the Lisa's Motorola 16-bit microprocessor into the nascent Macintosh, somehow getting it to run quicker and yet be cheaper to build. The promise of a cheap but powerful computer attracted the attention of Steve Jobs, who saw a chance to break the dominance of the IBM PC P. 66, and he started developing a Lisa-like graphical user interface. The result was a computer costing $2,495 with a monochrome 512-by-342-pixel display, a mouse, and programs such as MacWrite and MacPaint to demonstrate its core functionality.

The novelty of the Macintosh's operating system led to a lack of software support, although Microsoft became an important partner, releasing Word in early 1985. But Microsoft soon turned on Apple. The '1984' advert told a story of emancipation, of free creativity smashing away the yoke of grey dystopian conformity. Its symbolism was hard to miss: Apple was sticking one to IBM. But in reality, Apple had established its own brand of conformity. The Macintosh was a closed system, so developers had to buy a licence to write software for it. Microsoft saw an opportunity to use its influence to carve itself a better position: it threatened to stop making software for the Macintosh if Apple didn't give it a licence for the operating system. Worried, CEO John Sculley granted it, and in doing so allowed Microsoft to develop Windows without fear of Apple suing.

Within Apple, meanwhile, Jobs's position was souring. The Macintosh was selling slowly, and the Apple II P. 31 development group didn't like that Jobs was sidelining its work. The 512-KB model added much-needed RAM in September 1984, but Jobs lost control of the project a year later P. 221. Apple, meanwhile, realized the Macintosh's importance as the GUI became pervasive and as it started to transform industries such as desktop publishing. But Windows, running on IBM-compatibles, had been allowed to get the jump on it.

ORIGIN
United Kingdom

TECHNICAL DATA
Motorola 68008 at 7.5 MHz, 128 KB RAM

AVAILABLE
April 1984

MANUFACTURER
Sinclair Research

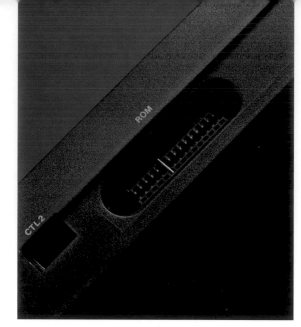

SINCLAIR QL

Until the QL, computers were simple and single-minded. Programs ran one at a time, or interrupted each other so that they could complete their jobs. But the QL could multitask, allotting chunks of time to every running process, giving the magical impression that they were running simultaneously and continuously. This sleight of hand, which still underpins every home computer today, was down to an operating system called QDOS designed by Sinclair Research software engineer Tony Tebby. It performed just what the QL's name implied: a quantum leap. But the computer itself was a disaster.

The QL was the product of Clive Sinclair's wish to build a computer for business. Codenamed ZX83, it was originally conceived in 1981 as a portable, but its ambitious specification, with which lead engineer David Karlin aimed to surpass the IBM PC, used a 16-bit Motorola 68000 microprocessor (or at least its chopped-down and cheaper 68008 variant), and soon turned the project into a desktop computer.

Keeping costs down while negotiating new technology brought about many problems, but the 16-bit era was dawning. Apple was poised to release the Macintosh P. 151, and Atari's ST P. 191 and Commodore's Amiga P. 195 weren't far behind. Anxious to keep ahead of them, Sinclair revealed the QL on 12 January 1984 – beating Apple's presentation of the Macintosh by twelve days – and began taking orders, promising shipment within a month. But as far as the QL's designers were concerned, it needed at least another six months' work. Its ULA chips weren't finished, and QDOS wouldn't be completed until March. First shipments to customers arrived weeks late, and they were unreliable: software didn't load, the system crashed, and there were no manuals. Part of the ROM came on an external cartridge. And the twin Microdrives were a mess.

Tebby resigned in protest at the chaotic launch, and even though this advanced system cost just £399, sales were low. Businesses wanted IBM PCs and their ecosystem of software, and the home market wanted games that the QL didn't have. What's more, although a 68000 cost three times as much as the 68008 when they chose to use it in the QL, the team was surprised to watch as their 16-bit competitors used the faster chip. Sinclair's cost- and time-pinching practices had undermined the QL's future-minded invention, and it was withdrawn from sale in 1985.

MANUFACTURER
Oric Products International

AVAILABLE
January 1984

TECHNICAL DATA
MOS 6502A at 1 MHz, 16 KB or 48 KB
RAM

ORIGIN
United Kingdom

With the Oric-1 P.97 only a year old, Oric Products International was skirting collapse. It had gained a foothold in the British home computer market, but the company's small scale just wasn't enough to sustain it. Enter Edenspring Investments, which offered to buy out Oric's owners in return for £4 million. Those funds would pay for an R&D centre in Cambridge to help Oric diversify outside computers into new tech businesses, such as medical instruments and business communications, and extend the runway for the release of a new home machine that would continue the Oric-1's momentum.

The Atmos looked very different to the little white computer that preceded it. Oric's hope was that the new case would help the market to forget the Oric-1's technical problems, particularly its buggy ROM. But inside the black facade and under its improved keyboard, the Atmos was much the same machine, now shipping with a largely – but not completely – fixed version 1.1 ROM (cassette loading commands could still be tricksy), and bringing together various fixes to the Oric-1's original logic board. Computing magazines were not fooled, but production accelerated, and at one point during 1984 Oric was making 10,000 Atmos computers a month. Like the Oric-1, the Atmos was particularly popular in France, and it was also licensed out to companies in Bulgaria and Yugoslavia.

Oric continued to design new computers, planning to release five by spring 1985, including an MSX-compatible and an IBM-compatible machine. But behind the scenes Oric was failing to pay its suppliers, including Pan Books, which had produced the Atmos manual. The company managed to launch only one new computer, the Stratos, on 1 February 1985 at the Frankfurt Computer Show. The very next day, Edenspring put Oric into receivership with estimated debts of £5.5 million and assets of £3.5 million. French company Eureka bought what remained of the company and supported the Stratos, releasing it in France as the Telestrat. Inside, it was yet another Oric-1 – this time with more memory. Against all the odds, that little machine turned out to be a remarkable survivor.

ORIC ATMOS

AMSTRAD CPC 464

ORIGIN
United Kingdom

TECHNICAL DATA
Zilog Z80A at 4 MHz, 64 KB RAM

AVAILABLE
June 1984

MANUFACTURER
Amstrad

From its founding in 1966 by bluff London entrepreneur Alan Sugar, Amstrad was all about selling electronics to the mass market. Sugar had spent the 1970s trading in cheap hi-fis and TVs, often importing them from East Asia and rebadging them. Quality and innovation weren't as important as price and demand, so it wasn't until the ZX Spectrum P.91 proved the home computer was a mass-market product that Amstrad became interested in making its own. It also helped that its traditional product lines were beginning to plateau.

That first computer was the CPC 464, and it went on to sell over two million units and redefine the company. The vision behind it showed a keen awareness of the place computers had in the home: in order to avoid taking over the family TV, the 464 would include a keyboard and tape records and be sold with a monitor. Also wallet-friendly, it was a winning concept, but development wasn't easy.

Since Amstrad had no experience of making computers, the company had to bring in outside expertise, while itself designing the computer's distinctive black casing and sourcing its keyboard and tape player. The two designers hired to develop the main board and write its ROM, whom Sugar described as 'a couple of long-haired hippies', underestimated the work involved. Having started on a 6502-based machine, one of them collapsed under the pressure, so in summer 1983 Amstrad found new designers: childhood friends William Poel and Roland Perry.

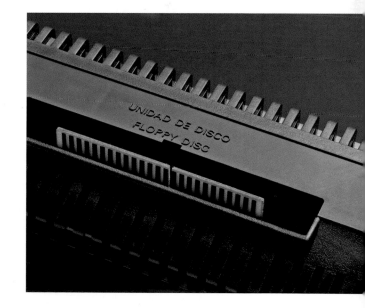

They pulled together the CPC 464, signing up a software developer to write its ROM and an engineer to create a Z80-powered board that would fit into the case Amstrad had already designed. They pushed each contractor to finish their work so they could complete the project on time; the board was complete in November, and even though its ULA chip wasn't finished until February, the team began sending prototypes to game developers in December. Despite the risk of the computer leaking to the public, Sugar knew that it needed plenty of games ready for its launch in June. The ploy worked: practical, functional, and available at £239 with a green monitor or £349 with a colour one, the 464 had immediate mass appeal. In Europe, anyway.

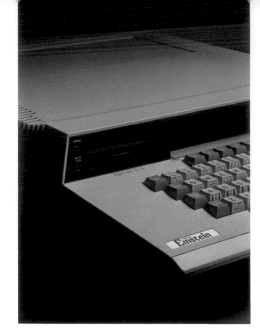

ORIGIN
United Kingdom

TECHNICAL DATA
Zilog Z80A at 4 MHz, 64 KB RAM

AVAILABLE
1984

MANUFACTURER
Tatung Corporation

It takes a special kind of confidence to name your computer after a Nobel Prize-winning physicist who defined a pillar of scientific thinking. In truth, the Tatung Einstein was yet another computer fitted with the ubiquitous Z80 processor and a reasonable amount of memory, and it didn't sell very well because it was priced at a rather expensive £499. But the Einstein was nevertheless quietly special.

Not that you would think so if you saw its specification. It wasn't compatible with the MSX format, but it shared the same microprocessor and video chip. In fact, it was so similar to the Memotech MTX series P. 143 that both could run an expansion board called the Speculator, which emulated a ZX Spectrum P. 91, and play a certain number of its games, including *Atic Atac* and Daley Thompson's *Decathlon*. They ran a little slower than on a native machine and the Speculator added a little extra flicker to their graphics, but it worked remarkably well. Some games were converted to the Einstein, too, including favourites such as *Jet Set Willy* and *Dragon's Lair*. But no one really saw the Einstein as a gaming machine. It was a game-making machine.

By the 1970s, Tatung was Taiwan's largest private company, but the Einstein was designed at its R&D division in Bradford in the north of England, and manufactured in Telford in the English Midlands. Tatung aimed to create a computer for small businesses, but managed instead to make one for programmers. That's because it booted directly into its Machine Operating System, which was so low-level that it gave programmers access to its deeper systems, allowing control over such components as its disk controller.

The result was that many game developers in the UK ended up using the Einstein to write games for other systems. They liked that they could rewrite its operating system to fit their needs, and that they could write assembler code for the Spectrum on an Einstein and then send it directly to a Spectrum to test it. What's more, they liked the Einstein's keyboard and its power supply, which could ride out mains fluctuations without the computer losing power.

TATUNG EINSTEIN TC-01

ORIGIN
United Kingdom

TECHNICAL DATA
Motorola 68008 at 7.5 MHz, 128 KB RAM

AVAILABLE
November 1984

MANUFACTURER
International Computers Limited

ICL MERLIN TONTO

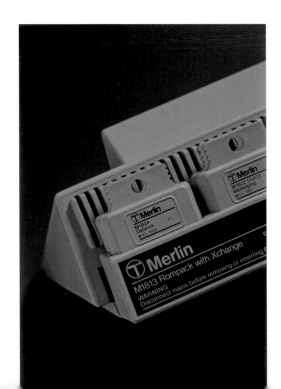

What kind of computer might come out of a collaboration between a celebrated consumer electronics firm, a mainframe manufacturer, and a national telecommunications company? The answer is a computer with a phone receiver sitting on top. Originally called the One Per Desk (OPD), it was the product of Sinclair Research, International Computers Limited, and British Telecom joining forces to make a workstation that could connect to other computers over a telephone line and form the basis of a new national set of online services.

Sold in the UK as the Merlin Tonto, and in Australia as the Telecom Computerphone, the OPD was largely a Sinclair QL P. 153 fitted with a V.21/V.23 modem and two telephone lines, so it could be attached to a network while taking voice calls. It also included a voice synthesizer, which could automatically take calls, and two Microdrives for storage. The original ZX Microdrive was, like so many Sinclair products, both clever and tooth-grindingly unreliable. It was capable of reading data at 15 KB per second, but its magnetic tape was prone to snarling up and sometimes riven with bad sectors. The Microdrive in the OPD, however, was based on the QL's version – which ran slower and thereby put the tape under less tension – and re-engineered by ICL for further reliability.

The OPD was entirely incompatible with the QL, since it ran its own operating system and the ICL Microdrive used a different format. Many OPDs were used by British Telecom itself. The machine was also used to drive the UK's National Bingo Game, in which clubs across the nation would call out numbers from the same lists. The OPD retrieved the numbers via its modem from the main server, which was operated by the National Bingo Association, and then it would send the winners' details back again to the main office so that prizes of up to £50,000 could be coordinated. When it launched in June 1986 the National Bingo Game was the UK's largest computer-controlled game, only surpassed by the National Lottery in 1994.

COMMODORE 116

ORIGIN
United States

TECHNICAL DATA
MOS 7501 at 0.89 MHz, 16 KB RAM

AVAILABLE
1984

MANUFACTURER
Commodore International

Even as the VIC-20 P.56 and 64 P.79 broke sales records, Jack Tramiel continued to worry that Japanese companies would begin exporting cheap microcomputers to the West and destroy all he had built at Commodore. Watching as cheap computers such as the Timex Sinclair P.124 hit the market and Texas Instruments cut the price of its TI-99/4A P.69, he decided that the VIC-20, now several years old, needed to be replaced by a stripped-down machine that could launch for between $50 and $80.

Tramiel was wrong. Japanese computers never took hold in North America and made little impact in Europe, and the Commodore 16, as it was known in the US, was a flop. It was underpowered and under-supported, and it launched at $99, way over Tramiel's price-point. But for principal engineer Bil Herd, the 16 was a faithful interpretation of Tramiel's difficult and ultimately misguided brief. It featured a newer and faster processor than the 6502 in the Commodore 64, and its 7360 Text Editing Device (TED) chip – hardware that also featured in its enhanced sibling, the Plus/4 P.166 – supported 121 colours.

One key problem was the 16's lack of software; it was short on business applications, and it was particularly underserved for games, too: it didn't support sprites, and it lacked the standard Commodore joystick ports because the usual connector was too big for its diminutive case. What's more, it only had 12 KB available for programs, making its conversions of popular titles such as *Ghosts 'n Goblins* and *Beach Head* the worst of any format.

In Europe, the 16 (known there as the 116) sold rather better. It featured an even smaller casing and a rubber chiclet keyboard with four separate cursor keys. The great majority of software released for the platform was made in Europe, even though the 116 was competing there with the rather more capable Spectrum. The flagship of the series, the Plus/4, would do little better.

ORIGIN
United States

TECHNICAL DATA
MOS 6510 at 1 MHz, 64 KB RAM

AVAILABLE
1984

MANUFACTURER
Commodore Business Machines

COMMODORE SX-64

The first colour portable computer was essentially a Commodore 64 **P. 79**. The suitcase-shaped, 10.5-kg SX-64 was a full makeover of Commodore's doughty brown home computer. The company hoped that the SX-64 would become indispensable for the globe-trotting businessperson; it was called the 'Executive' and priced at nearly $1,000 to prove it.

The SX-64's keyboard was stowed on the end to protect the screen and the Commodore 1541 floppy-disk drive, in a design very similar to Compaq's Portable **P. 120**, which had launched the previous year, and the Osborne **P. 65** before it. But it wasn't a thoughtless copy: the SX-64 featured a width-long handle that turned to form a stand for the main unit, inclining its end upwards to make its tiny 5-in. CRT screen more visible. To render the screen more readable, the SX-64 reversed the 64's classic scheme of white text on a blue background.

But this clever design wasn't enough to alleviate the screen's size, which didn't measure up to the generous 9 in. of Compaq's Portable. Moreover, the BASIC-based SX-64 didn't quite have the same business credentials as a DOS-based IBM-compatible (and the software that came with it), and although the Commodore 64 was a very capable games machine, its processor didn't perform on the executive level of the Portable's Intel 8088.

Also hanging over the SX-64 was the fact that Commodore had already announced the DX-64, a model with dual floppy drives that never ended up being released. The SX-64 consequently didn't sell very well, with estimates suggesting it shifted fewer than 10,000 units. It was discontinued in 1986.

Commodore SX-64, cary handle ↑

ORIGIN
United States

TECHNICAL DATA
MOS 7501 at 0.89 MHz, 64 KB RAM

AVAILABLE
1984

MANUFACTURER
Commodore International

Jack Tramiel seemed to be riding high at the January 1984 Consumer Electronics Show in Las Vegas. He took to the stage to announce that Commodore had earned over a billion dollars in revenue the previous year and showed off a new series of computers, the 264 family, which included the Commodore 16 P. 163. But he abruptly left the company a few days later. Was he edged out because his uncompromising business style was alienating partners? Was he also alienating Commodore's own staff? Was he was too controlling, insisting on signing off every expense over $1,000? What's certain is that by the time the cut-price 264 family had proved Commodore's first computer failure, Tramiel was long gone.

The Plus/4 was 264's flagship. Marketed to businesses as a comprehensive office computer, it came with a ROM packed with a word processor, spreadsheet, and database. They were based on Pacific Tri-Micro's TRILOGY, and because they were stored in ROM, they loaded much faster than they would have from tape – but they were universally disliked. Canadian Commodore magazine *The Transactor* said, 'The word processor is barely that, the data base defiles the name, and the spreadsheet has little spread.'

Without Tramiel at the head of the company, the Plus/4 lost much of its focus on price. It launched at an inflated $300 and struggled to attract new business software; most software it had access to was made for the 16's 16-KB RAM, and thus didn't take advantage of the Plus/4's greater memory. Many different versions were launched, each attempting to find a niche for the computer, but ultimately its main competition was the older but more appealing Commodore 64 P.79.

However, it did find a foothold in central Europe. Forced to dump stocks, Commodore sold the Plus/4 at a heavy discount there, and it became Hungary's official school computer. Around it grew a big programming and publishing scene, which converted hit Commodore 64 games and wrote original software for a machine that, elsewhere, had long since been superseded.

COMMODORE PLUS/4

MANUFACTURER
Microdigital Electrónica

AVAILABLE
1985

TECHNICAL DATA
Zilog Z80A at 3.6 MHz, 16 KB–48 KB RAM

ORIGIN
Brazil

Between 1964 and 1985, Brazil was a repressive military dictatorship, but that couldn't quash the Brazilian fascination for home computers. As a measure to build up local industry, the Brazilian government had made it illegal to import computer hardware and software for which there was a Brazilian equivalent, so, without any way of selling real ZX81s **P. 71**, TRS-80s **P. 53** and Apple IIs **P. 31**, Brazilian companies such as Microdigital turned to making copies, including the TK80, a clone of the ZX80 **P. 48**, and the TK3000, a clone of the Apple IIe.

The TK90X was a clone of the ZX Spectrum **P. 91**, compatible with around 90 per cent of Spectrum software because its ROM was slightly modified, with Portuguese translation and new commands such as TRACE and UDG (user-defined graphics). The hardware was somewhat improved, featuring a better heatsink and the ability to channel sound to a TV rather than playing it through the built-in speaker.

By the time it was making the TK90X, Microdigital was a serious electronics outfit with four hundred workers across three factories, and it exported its computers across Latin America. Naturally, Sinclair Research wasn't happy with its products being copied, and it started a lawsuit on the production of the TK82C, a clone of the ZX81. But Sinclair lost. Brazil didn't recognize international copyright for software, and because Sinclair hadn't previously registered the ZX81's ROM for copyright in Brazil, Microdigital hadn't contravened anything by copying it. What's more, while the judge agreed that the first 12 KB of the ROM was identical to Sinclair's original, the last 4 KB (which had been modified, like the TK90X's, with new commands and translations) was different. It ruled, therefore, that the ROM wasn't a straight copy.

The TK90X was succeeded in 1986 by the TK95, which was more compatible with Spectrum software and featured a full-travel keyboard, but it was to be the last computer made by Microdigital. The company had missed the quick rise of the MSX format and had fallen behind the times. By the end of the 1980s the trade restrictions on computers were lifted, and trade in copied systems became subject to international law.

MICRODIGITAL TK90X

ORIGIN
United Kingdom

TECHNICAL DATA
Z80A at 3.5 MHz, 128 KB RAM

AVAILABLE
September 1985

MANUFACTURER
Sinclair Research

As Sinclair Research followed up on the ZX Spectrum's P. 91 market-swelling success, it worked on a number of skunkworks projects. Many that penetrated the public consciousness were cancelled, such as the LC3 (a ZX81 P. 71 with colour display) and the superlatively named SuperSpectrum, which was meant to be powered by a Motorola 68008 and feature every add-on a child could dream of. But some did see store shelves, even if they seemed rather hurried and conservative. The first was the Spectrum+ in October 1984, which replaced the original and featured a much friendlier plastic keyboard. It was, however, reported by some retailers to have a failure rate that might have been as high as 30 per cent.

The 128K launched a year later. Despite dominating the market of the mid-1980s, Sinclair Research was not cash-rich. The QL P. 153 had failed, and the constant need to reduce the Spectrum's price so it could continue competing in the market was cutting heavily into profits. So when Sinclair's Spanish distributor Investrónica offered to invest in a new computer designed for the Spanish market, Sinclair leapt at the chance. The aim was to address, as quickly as possible, some of the Spectrum's deficiencies as a gaming computer. The 128K's most obvious upgrade was its RAM. It was also given 128 BASIC, which finally dumped the old keyword command input system and added the SPECTRUM command to switch the computer to 48-KB mode for full compatibility with the older system. It also added three-channel sound and MIDI, and switched the original Spectrum's much-derided beeper for a proper speaker.

Of course, in order to use these features, games had to be written specifically for the 128K. Most were quick and dirty ports of 48-KB versions, but some were more considered, such as *Starglider*, which added missions, a scanner, replays, and speech. Time, however, was catching up with Sinclair. The 128K was released in Spain in September 1985 at 44,250 pesetas, but it wasn't available in the UK until the following January because Sinclair had so much unsold Spectrum+ stock. Four months later, Amstrad would buy all Sinclair's computer assets. It carried on supporting the Spectrum through incrementally improved versions such as the +3, which continued to be built until 1990. Sinclair Research returned to R&D, but never had another hit.

SINCLAIR SPECTRUM 128K

MANUFACTURER
Amstrad

AVAILABLE
September 1985

TECHNICAL DATA
Zilog Z80A at 4 MHz, 128 KB RAM

ORIGIN
United Kingdom

In the months following the CPC 464's P. 157 launch, Amstrad proved a careful custodian of its newfound success as a computer maker. It supported the 464 with a disk drive add-on and a version of the CP/M operating system, and unlike every other manufacturer, it refused to drop its price – even in May 1985 when it released the CPC 664, which came with an integrated 3½-in. disk drive but retailed at £100 more than the 464.

The 664 only enjoyed a short life. Just two months after its release, the CPC 6128 arrived with 128 KB of RAM, the same disk drive, and a more subdued business-casual style. In fact, the 6128 was designed for the US market, where the 464 hadn't sold well. But British retailers immediately wanted it too, and so in September 1985 Amstrad gave it to them. For those who hadn't run out to buy a 664, it was fantastic news: it cost £229 for the green-monitor model and £399 for colour, prices that ran slightly lower than the 464 had commanded at launch. Amstrad quietly withdrew the 664 and finally reduced the price of the 464 to £199 for the green-monitor model and £299 for colour.

While 664 owners were left feeling out of pocket, the 6128 offered exactly the right value for an imploding market in which new companies, from Jupiter Cantab P. 93 to Dragon Data P. 95, were failing, and even large and established ones, such as Acorn, were faltering. Once again, Amstrad had known what was needed for the market, and provided it fast. With a fast-growing stable of games and applications, the 6128 was perhaps the best-value 8-bit home computer released, selling well in the UK, France, Germany, and Spain. But although some games, such as Virgin's platformer adventure *Sorcery+*, were enhanced for its larger RAM, most game makers didn't bother, afraid of cutting support for the more widespread 464.

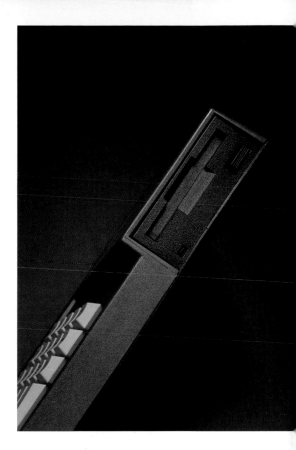

AMSTRAD CPC 6128

MANUFACTURER
Enterprise Computers

AVAILABLE
June 1985

TECHNICAL DATA
Zilog Z80A at 4 MHz, 128 KB RAM

ORIGIN
United Kingdom

ENTERPRISE
ONE TWO EIGHT

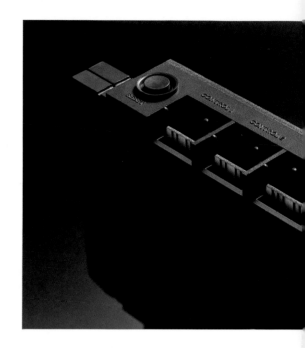

It takes a particular kind of vision to design a computer and call two of its chips Nick and Dave. In the case of the Enterprise, these chips were the source of its high-end graphics and memory, and were named, of course, after their designers. Nick (Toop) powered its graphics, which could drive remarkably high-resolution 672-by-5120-pixel colour graphics, albeit interlaced. Dave (Woodfield) controlled the computer's sound and memory paging, which allowed its Z80 to access a remarkably voluminous maximum of 4 MB of RAM.

Of course, the Enterprise was a flop. Along with its stablemate, the Sixty Four, the One Two Eight came out too late, the victim of protracted development that began all the way back in 1982, just after the ZX Spectrum P. 91 was launched. David Levy of chess AI maker Intelligent Software was approached by a Hong Kong-based backer to create a computer to rival Sinclair's hit, and so Levy and a band of engineers set out to build the best home computer on the market. The company announced the computer in September 1983, despite trouble giving it a name. It started as DPC (standing for Damp Proof Course, a codename designed to flummox leaks), Samurai (clashed with a standing trademark), Oscar (no one liked it), Elan (another trademark clash), and, incredibly, Flan (because on paper it looked like Elan), before finally arriving at Enterprise. In Germany it was known as the Mephisto.

The machine gathered plenty of attention – preorders in early 1984 stood at over 80,000 – partly for its high-end specifications and partly for its design. The Enterprise's keyboard and curved casing, complete with joystick, were designed by Nick Oakley and Geoff Hollington, who designed pens for Parker, furniture for Herman Miller, and the Je Joue vibrator. Its rounded keys were inspired by Olivetti's Italian typewriters, although its accented use of colour was foisted on it later and looked uncomfortably close to the scheme used by Amstrad's CPC 464 P. 157. But the Enterprise ended up badly delayed. The Sixty Four emerged in February 1985 with a higher-than-planned price (£180) and not enough software. Its technical ingenuity and style were largely forgotten, and the great majority of its stock ended up being sold abroad, particularly in Hungary.

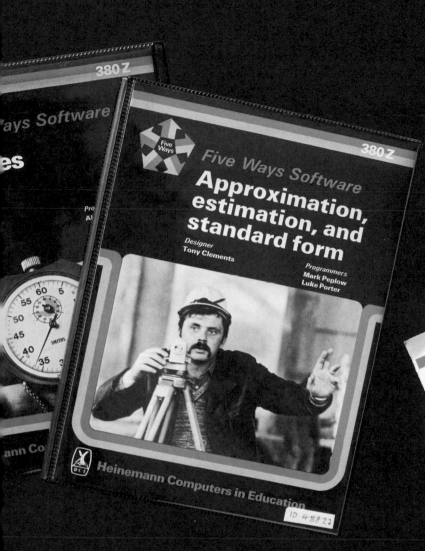

While practical software and hardware tended
to be sold on their technical properties, games
had to sell themselves on fun. The key way to
do so was with rich and colourful covers hinting
at the action that existed on the other side of a
few minutes' worth (or more) of loading screens.
Naturally, the pixelated reality never quite aligned
with the cover image, but the painted scenes
often served to fill in the imaginative gaps in the
games themselves, making the cover an indelible
part of the whole experience.

Research Machines 380Z educational
software packages

Enterprise marketing brochure

Aquarius 4-KB memory cartridge packaging

Tandy 1000 EX MS-DOS software

Acorn RISC OS 3
Applications disc 2

Insert this way up

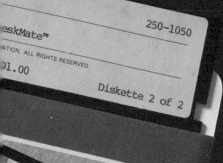

eskMate™   250–1050

ATION, ALL RIGHTS RESERVED

01.00   Diskette 2 of 2

1000 EX

MS-DOS ® / GW™ —BASIC   Drive A

Cat No. 25-1050
Diskette 1 of 2

ACORNSOFT GAMES

Sphinx Adventu
for the BBC Microcomputer Mode

Acorn Archimedes RISC OS 3
applications disks

BBC Micro *Sphinx Adventure* game

Amstrad CPC 464 software

Aquarius *Night Stalker* game

Commodore Amiga
Sensible Soccer game

Amstrad joypad and *Burnin' Rubber*
game cartridge

ORIC

SOFTWARE

WELCOME TO ORIC

VIC-20
COLOUR COMPUTER

CARTRIDGE

AVENGER

Oric-1 welcome software

Commodore VIC-20 *Avenger* game

NEXTSTEP software

Acorn Archimedes *Chocks Away* game

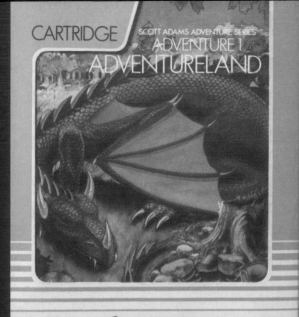

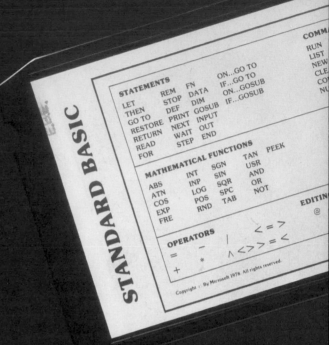

Commodore VIC-20 *Adventureland* game

Exidy Sorcerer BASIC cartridge

Atari ST *The Chaos Engine* game

ORIGIN
United States

TECHNICAL DATA
MOS 6502C at 1.8 MHz, 64 KB RAM

AVAILABLE
February 1985

MANUFACTURER
Atari Corporation

When Jack Tramiel suddenly left Commodore after revealing the 264 series, including the Plus/4 P. 166, in January 1984, he didn't take much of a holiday. In May he founded a new company, Tramel Technology, to build new computers, and by July he had bought Atari's consumer division. Atari: his old competitor. 1983 had been an *annus horribilis* for Atari, in no small part because of the price war that Tramiel had done so much to spur, and it had accrued losses that led its parent, Warner Communications, to put it up for sale.

Tramiel saw a perfect opportunity to start afresh by buying Atari, along with its worldwide manufacturing resources. On taking the helm, he immediately applied his head for strategy and his focus on low price-points, not to mention his personal history, having grown up in Poland. As he watched the Soviet Union begin to break up, he saw fresh markets emerging in the newly independent Eastern European nations, which were hungry for cheap computers. And so Atari produced two, the 65XE and 130XE. They might have looked like Atari STs P. 191, but the 65XE was in fact more or less a simple rehousing of the 800XL P. 129; the 130XE was the same, but with 128 KB of RAM. Of course, the important thing about them was not their specification but their price: the 65XE was just $99.99. Announced alongside the ST, it was designed to be the budget option in a wide product range for Tramiel's new Atari.

Atari continued to build the XE computers until 1991, after the Soviet Union finally dissolved, and they sold well. In Germany and Czechoslovakia the 65XE was badged as the 800XE to capitalize on strong sales of the 800XL there. Atari's 8-bit computers, from the 400 and 800 P. 40 to the 65XE and XE Game System console, were in production until 1992 and sold some four million units in total. Over that time, the fundamentals of their internals barely changed, a testament to the robustness of the original design.

ATARI 65XE

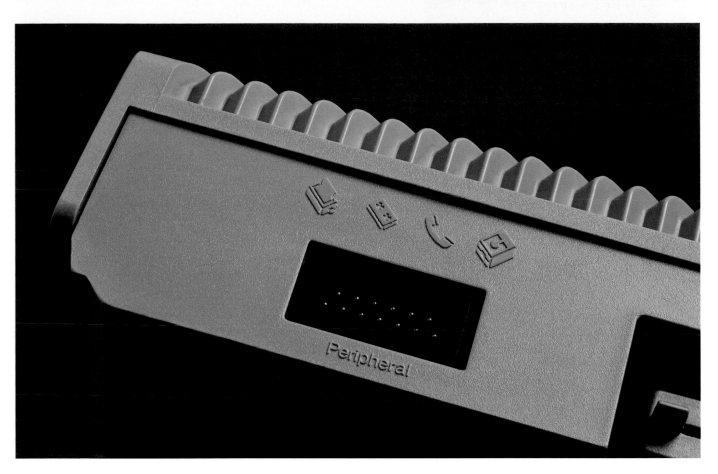

ORIGIN
United States

TECHNICAL DATA
MOS 8502 at 2 MHz and Zilog Z80B
at 2 MHz, 128 KB RAM

AVAILABLE
1985

MANUFACTURER
Commodore Business Machines

As 1985 dawned, Commodore's grip on the computer industry was slipping. It might have won the home computer price wars, but Apple had kicked off a new generation in user-friendly interface design, along with a jump to a new generation of microprocessors, while IBM's PC was gathering more and more momentum. What's more, former CEO Jack Tramiel was deep into planning a new computer at his new company, Atari. With its own 16-bit computer still months away, Commodore's answer, for the moment, was the Commodore 128.

This Commodore 64 P. 79 successor aimed to take advantage of two vast bodies of software that were popular at the time. For those who hadn't yet finished with the Commodore 64 and all the games and applications written for it, the 128 had a MOS 8502 microprocessor, which gave it almost complete compatibility while also being able to run at double the clock speed and with extra colours granted by its extra video RAM. And for those who wanted a computer for the office, the 128 featured a Zilog Z80B, which allowed it to support the CP/M operating system and its huge library of business applications.

Unsurprisingly, this attempt to make one computer for two purposes presented some caveats. On one hand, the 8502 wasn't really able to run at full speed because its VIC-II video chip couldn't keep up with it, so most of the time it ran at half speed. And for CP/M, the 128 ran rather slower than most other Z80-based machines, since its microprocessor was throttled by the 128's 6502-based system bus. Many applications written for its 8502-powered C128 mode, such as word processor Paperclip, ran quicker than their CP/M counterparts.

Although the Commodore Amiga P. 195 was released at the end of the year, Commodore also released revised models of the 128, including the 128D, which separated the keyboard from the main body, and the 128DCR, which greatly upgraded the video chip. And although it was under-supported by software makers, who were more interested in making games and applications for the new generation, the 128 sold some four million units over its lifetime. Nevertheless, it stood very much in the shadow of the Amiga.

COMMODORE 128

Commodore 128, top panel, detail ↑

MANUFACTURER
Atari Corporation

AVAILABLE
September 1985

TECHNICAL DATA
Motorola 68000 at 8 MHz; 512 KB
or 1 MB RAM

ORIGIN
United States

ATARI
520 ST FM

Jack Tramiel began planning a next-generation computer only a few weeks after he left Commodore, but it wasn't until he bought Atari that he had the ideal infrastructure to manufacture, market, and distribute it. Once established as the leader of the company that had once been his competitor, Tramiel started to bring engineers and executives across from Commodore, including Shiraz Shivji, who had worked on the Commodore 64 and would lead development on the computer that became the Atari ST. Naturally, Commodore, realizing it was losing the talent it needed to build its own next-generation computer, began filing lawsuits for theft of trade secrets, and a bitter war started between the two companies.

An important battleground was a company called Amiga, which had been founded by ex-Atari employees Jay Miner and Larry Kaplan. Amiga was designing a next-generation computer codenamed Lorraine, which it had shown off in January 1984 with a demo of an apparently 3D ball. While it stunned crowds, few buyers came knocking. Atari, however, wondered rather idly if Lorraine could perhaps form the basis for a new game console. In March, Amiga began to run out of money and, with the aim of sustaining its interest in the project, Atari offered it a one-month loan of $500,000 with the proviso that if Amiga was late in repaying, it had to give Lorraine away as forfeit. Commodore, meanwhile, had realized that Amiga could be the source of its new computer. In August 1984 it bought the company for $24 million, and sent Atari $500,000 to end the loan arrangement. In return, Tramiel, hoping to prevent Commodore from using Lorraine, unsuccessfully sued Amiga.

Atari knew that Lorraine had given Commodore a huge head-start on its next-generation computer, so all efforts went towards showing off the 520 ST at CES in January 1985. Much of the reaction focused on its seemingly cheap build quality. Indeed, on its launch at the end of summer, the machine was criticized for reliability issues and for having very little software: hallmarks of rushed development. But the 520 ST's reasonably powerful specification and TOS, its mouse-driven graphical operating system, still captured attention, particularly in Europe. The Amiga, however, was hot on its heels, and it would prove that the ST's sprint to market did it few favours.

Atari 520 ST FM, joystick and mouse ports, keyboard detail.

ORIGIN
United States

TECHNICAL DATA
Motorola 68000 at 7.1 MHz, 256 KB RAM

AVAILABLE
October 1985

MANUFACTURER
Commodore International

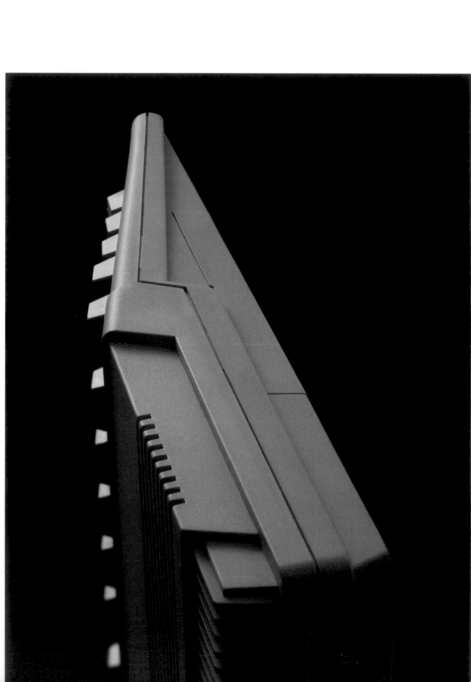

COMMODORE
AMIGA 1000

When Larry Kaplan, cofounder of the game publisher Activision, was approached by investors interested in funding a next-generation gaming system in 1982, he in turn approached a fellow Atari alumni called Jay Miner to design it. Miner had designed the video chips in the Atari 2600, 400, and 800 and was frustrated that Atari wouldn't let him build a new system around Motorola's new 16-bit 68000 microprocessor. Together they formed a new company called Hi-Toro, where they developed a 16-bit computer motherboard that they codenamed Lorraine.

Kaplan left in late 1982, whereupon the company renamed itself Amiga, and over the next year it developed powerful system hardware and an operating system, releasing joysticks and add-ons for consoles to keep funds flowing. However, after Amiga revealed Lorraine at CES in January 1984 and failed to find a buyer, its financial troubles became acute – until Commodore, seeing Lorraine as the basis for its new next-generation computer, swept in and bought the company in August.

The Amiga 1000 launched a year later at an event during which Andy Warhol painted Debbie Harry on one of the machines to demonstrate its potential for digital art. It was the first real multimedia computer, able to display up to 4,096 colours on screen at a 320-by-200-pixel resolution, a fact on which Commodore's marketing fixated. The 1000's power and price certainly easily outpaced the Atari 520 ST P. 191 and IBM-compatible PCs, partly down to its history as a gaming system. It ran with thoroughbred efficiency that resulted from a clock speed tuned to exactly double its video frequency, and memory access synchronized so that no component had to halt momentarily in a wait state.

The 1000 also came with AmigaOS, a powerful GUI-based multitasking operating system. But Commodore struggled to place the computer in the marketplace of 1985. On the one hand, 256 KB of RAM was definitely on the low side for professional users. On the other, $1,295 was expensive for a home system, and the 1000 couldn't connect to a TV. It was a few months before units were actually supplied to buyers, but the Amiga did, in fact, became the backbone of real-time computer graphics professionals. However, its real impact wouldn't come until the cheaper 500 P. 244 was released in 1987.

MANUFACTURER
Matra Hachette

AVAILABLE
1985

TECHNICAL DATA
Motorola 6803 at 1 MHz, 32 KB RAM

ORIGIN
France

Alice 90

The Matra Alice P. 136 was followed in early 1984 by two versions with much-needed extra RAM. The Alice 32 featured 16 KB, as well as a Thomson EF9345 video chip that could display eight colours, a much more full-featured Microsoft BASIC editor, and a tape player in matching red. But Matra still couldn't find the mass market that it was after, so a few months later it released the Alice 90.

This time Matra chose a more angular look, slicing off the top left and bottom right corners, and replaced the chiclet keyboard with a full-travel one. The Alice 90 exchanged some of the toy-like charm of the original for a more technical approach, but inside it was just the Alice 32 with 32 KB of RAM. That is, apart from a video-in plug on its video cable that allowed it to overlay its graphics on an external video signal. Users could therefore use it to watch TV while programming: a precursor, perhaps, to a future generation attempting to concentrate while running YouTube.

Once again, it didn't catch on, and the Alice story finally ended later in 1985, when Matra designed a computer originally codenamed the Nanomachine and later renamed the Alice 8000. It was equipped with an Intel 8088 microprocessor, more memory, an integrated green-screen monitor, and white casing; Matra intended it to fit a bid to win a French government contract to place its computers in schools. Unfortunately for Matra, fellow French electronics corporation Thomson won with machines such as the MO6 P. 199, and only a few Alice 8000s actually emerged into the market. Defeated, Matra finally gave up on the microcomputer.

MATRA ALICE 90

MANUFACTURER
Thomson Micro-Informatique

AVAILABLE
September 1986

TECHNICAL DATA
Motorola 6809E at 1 MHz, 128 KB RAM

ORIGIN
France

Thomson believed that the home computer was a device for education, not games. 'If the micro is only a gaming machine, in a few years there will be no more family microcomputer,' Jean Gerothwohl, head of its computer group, told French computer news magazine *Soft & Micro* in 1984. So although the MO6 looked a little like a game-friendly MSX, it wasn't one. Besides, Gerothwohl didn't want to follow other standards. He knew that the 16-bit era was coming, and he wanted to establish a European standard that wouldn't be subject to heavy import taxes. The MO6, then, was something of a stopgap, designed to hold the line and appeal to schools and progressive parents until Thomson could build the next generation.

Thomson made many 6809E-powered 8-bit computers, in a series often referred to as MOTO. The first prototype was developed in 1979, and the first to see release was the TO7 in 1982, but Thomson wasn't particularly successful until the mid-1980s, when it won the contract to provide the hardware for the Informatique Pour Tous (IPT) programme, which was launched in 1985 to put computers into every school. Although IPT's founder, Jean-Jacques Servan-Schreiber, preferred Apple's Macintosh P.151 for the contract, and Apple had promised to establish a new factory in France as part of the deal, politics won out. As a nationalized company that was, frankly, struggling, Thomson was chosen instead.

The most common school computer was Thomson's MO5, often equipped with a 'nano network' add-on that allowed it to be networked in classrooms, but the MO6, with its greater RAM and new graphics modes, was also widespread. Unfortunately, Thomson never managed to rally European computer manufacturers around a new 16-bit standard. Although the company built a prototype all-in-one that ran on a Motorola 68000 processor and featured a multitasking operating system, its next and final computer was the IBM-compatible TO16, which launched in 1987. It sold half the volume Thomson expected, and the division went bankrupt in 1989.

THOMSON MO6

ORIGIN
Japan

TECHNICAL DATA
Zilog Z80A at 3.6 MHz, 16 KB RAM

AVAILABLE
1986

MANUFACTURER
Casio Computer Co.

MSX never managed to challenge the biggest computer formats, despite the popularity that saw it sell some nine million units in Japan and become common in countries all over the world, from Argentina to Cuba, South Korea to Kuwait, and the Netherlands to Spain. The trouble was that it didn't make inroads into the US and UK, where the biggest-selling computers were produced – but that didn't stop the MSX from evolving. When the MSX2 standard was established in 1985, it extended RAM and video RAM to at least 64 KB each, and replaced the TMS9918 video chip with the better and backwards-compatible Yamaha V9938. As a result, MSX2 computers supported more video modes, with more colours and greater resolution.

Despite being released in 1986, Casio's MX-10 was an MSX rather than an MSX2 machine. Casio focused on minimizing price and size, stripping out the usual tape interface and giving it just 16 KB of RAM and a nasty rubber keyboard. It also produced an interesting variant called the MX-101, which could broadcast its video signal over UHF using built-in antennas. Wireless computing had arrived, albeit briefly.

Casio had a knack for small-scale innovation. It was founded in 1946 by Tadao Kashio, who used the fortune he had made inventing a cigarette holder that allowed wearers to smoke right down to the end without burning their fingers (ideal for cash-strapped post-war Japan) to begin producing electro-mechanical calculators. By the 1980s, Casio was also known for its digital watches and keyboards, but computers were a natural fit; it released a succession of MSX, CP/M and DOS-compatible machines, plus a couple of game consoles, although they never replaced its core business.

ASCII released the MSX2+ specification in 1988, upgrading the video chip again, and then the final generation, the MSX TurboR, in 1990. TurboR ditched the Z80 in favour of a 16-bit microprocessor made by ASCII itself, but although it ran older MSX games smoothly, little software was written specifically for it. The market was waiting for MSX3, but it would never arrive. Its planned Yamaha video chip was delayed, and PCs and consoles took over the Japanese market.

CASIO MX-10 TYPE B

MANUFACTURER
Apple Computer

AVAILABLE
September 1986

TECHNICAL DATA
WDC 65C816 at 2.8 MHz,
256 KB–1 MB RAM

ORIGIN
United States

Apple celebrated its tenth anniversary by releasing the final main computer in the Apple II P. 31 line. Not that it really looked or behaved like one. Its keyboard was separate to its main unit, and it booted into a graphical operating system that looked a lot like the one in the Macintosh. Inside it ran a true 16-bit processor that could compete with the Amiga P. 195 and ST P. 191. And yet it was entirely compatible with software made for previous Apple II models, because its WDC microprocessor could emulate the 6502.

The first 50,000 units had Steve Wozniak's autograph silkscreened onto their front panels, in recognition of the engineer who had designed Apple's first computer and led every major project since. But Wozniak had left Apple twice before the IIGS released. In February 1981, Wozniak crashed his plane just after taking off and was left with concussion-related amnesia. After recovering, he decided to go his own way. He got married and organized two music and technology festivals called Unite Us in Song, but in 1983, after having lost several million dollars, he rejoined Apple and began working on a new computer called the Apple IIX, which used WDC's new 65816 processor.

But the IIX got bogged down. The processor was supplied late, and a desire to make it widely compatible with various coprocessors made it overly complicated. As a 16-bit computer, the IIX also clashed with the Macintosh P. 151, and so it was canned in March 1985. Wozniak moved on to new things – including the Apple Desktop Bus, which connected devices to computers – until he finally decided to leave Apple for good, frustrated that it wasn't letting him do enough engineering. He went on to complete a degree in electrical engineering and computer science at UC Berkley (enrolling as Rocky Raccoon Clark to avoid his fame gaining attention).

Apple, meanwhile, had decided to resurrect the IIX as the IIGS, which shipped with a deliberately slow clock speed so that it wouldn't outpace the Macintosh. Wozniak's Apple Desktop Bus saw its debut in the machine, connecting its mouse and keyboard with a standard that remained until the advent of USB in 1998. It was a quiet swansong for Wozniak's work on a seminal range of computers, but a swansong nonetheless.

APPLE IIGS

ORIGIN
United States

TECHNICAL DATA
Intel 8088 at 4.77 MHz, 256 KB RAM

AVAILABLE
December 1986

MANUFACTURER
Tandy Corporation

TANDY
1000 EX

Tandy's TRS-80 **P.27** series continued to sell into the 1980s with two basic lines: a series of expensive computers for business and the cheap CoCo **P.53** computers for homes, as well as a couple of portables. Each was incompatible with the other, but the market was changing. The IBM-compatible PC was taking hold, and it pointed towards a future in which standardization was a key selling point.

In March 1984, IBM released the PCjr, a PC aimed at the home market with a lower price and improved graphics and sound to support games such as the first *King's Quest*. It sold badly – its chiclet keyboard was terrible, its price was too high, and it wasn't fully IBM-compatible – but Tandy took a lot of notice of it, figuring that if it could copy the PCjr and iron out its problems, it would have a hit on its hands. The result was the supremely beige and boxy Tandy 1000, which Tandy released at the end of 1984 at $1,200 with a proper keyboard, better compatibility, and 'Tandy-compatible' (TGA) graphics and sound.

Little about the Tandy 1000 was by any means outstanding, but it was supported by Radio Shack, Tandy's own nation-spanning retailer. Well-marketed, keenly priced, and available everywhere, it was the right computer in the right place at the right time. It certainly helped that the Tandy 1000 was a very capable gaming machine. IBM wasn't awfully keen on its business-minded computers being associated with such frivolity, but Tandy embraced games, and its TGA standard supported sixteen colours (rather than the IBM CGA standard's four), while its sound chip supported three voices. The 1000's success led to TGA becoming a commonly supported standard among such classic PC titles as *The Bard's Tale* and *Where in the World is Carmen Sandiego?*

Tandy released many models, including the 1000 EX, which exchanged the original's IBM-like beige box and separate keyboard for a more slimline unit with an integrated keyboard. It came with MS-DOS 2.11 and Personal Deskmate, a mouse-driven suite of various applications and tools for the home. But it was the last computer line the company would make.

Detail, Tandy 1000 EX, power switch ↑

MANUFACTURER
Amstrad

AVAILABLE
October 1986

TECHNICAL DATA
Intel 8086 at 8 MHz, 512 KB RAM

ORIGIN
United Kingdom

It took Amstrad only two years to carve itself a space in the computer industry so strong that it could simply absorb its main competitor. In April 1986, it bought the worldwide rights to 'sell and manufacture all existing and future Sinclair computers and computer products'. With that, Amstrad became the biggest computer manufacturer in Europe, but it wasn't finished growing yet. A month later, Amstrad announced it was working on an IBM-compatible PC. By the early 1990s, Amstrad had shipped twelve million of them.

Once again, Amstrad had cornered a vast chunk of the market, not by being first to market or making the best computer, but by making a cheap computer at just the right time. The PC might have been ascendant in the US, but in 1986 it still hadn't made major inroads in Europe, and there were few inexpensive options available by the time the 1512 was launched. Full-featured and with a base model that cost just £399, including monitor, it was half the price of similarly powered PCs. The 1512 was hard to ignore, especially as it supported various expansions: the SD model featured a single disk drive, while the DD featured two, and both could come with a 10-MB or 20-MB hard disk.

The 1512's cheapness led to some issues, particularly with the fanless design of initial units. Although unconfirmed, rumours circulated that it was prone to overheating, leading Amstrad to begin installing fans to quell such fears despite there being no power supply in the main body of the computer. But despite cutting every cost it could, Amstrad ensured the 1512 was nothing less than a useful machine. It licensed MS-DOS 3.2 and also DOS Plus, which combined CP/M and DOS into a single operating system that gave a degree of support for both. The 1512 also shipped with GEM, a graphical operating system made by CP/M maker Digital Research **P. 37**. Its first version, released in 1985, looked so similar to Apple's Lisa **P. 146** and Macintosh **P. 151** operating systems that Apple sued, causing later versions of GEM to be restricted to two windows and animations for windows to be removed. Nevertheless, GEM provided the 1512's millions of owners with a taste of the future.

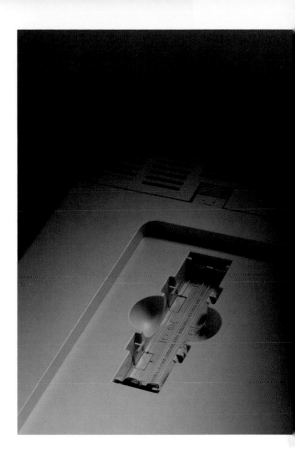

AMSTRAD PC1512 DD

Amstrad PC1512 DD, detail ↑

ORIGIN
United Kingdom

TECHNICAL DATA
Zilog Z80A at 4 MHz, 256 KB RAM

AVAILABLE
1986

MANUFACTURER
Tatung Corporation

TATUNG EINSTEIN 256

The Einstein P. 158 didn't sell very well, but Tatung was determined to support it, publishing a user magazine and software and updating it with a souped-up version, the 256, in 1986. Inside its slimmed-down black case (a great improvement on the vast chassis of the original), the 256 featured 256 KB of RAM and a Yamaha V9938 video chip.

Just as the original Einstein followed the MSX format, the 256 followed the MSX2 format P. 200, but it retained compatibility with almost all software written for its predecessor. That meant that the 256 made 64 KB available to programs and gave the remaining 192 KB to video, allowing it a maximum display resolution of 512 by 424 pixels, and up to 512 colours. Tatung accordingly supplied the machine with its own 14-in. colour monitor, which also provided the computer with power.

Once again, Tatung had made a computer with a high-quality build and speed that proved popular among programmers. Aside from pure game development, its Machine Operating System (MOS) allowed them to load specific disk sectors and then edit them before writing them back to disk. Coupled with the fact that the MOS gave control over the disk controller chip, this was a perfect way of writing copy protection systems in order to combat the software piracy that was rife at the time. But the 256 failed to break the pattern established by its predecessor, and once it was granted a licence, Tatung turned to producing IBM-compatible computers.

Tatung Einstein 256, top panel, detail ↑

MANUFACTURER
Acorn Computers

AVAILABLE
February 1986

TECHNICAL DATA
MOS 65SC12 at 2 MHz, 128 KB RAM

ORIGIN
United Kingdom

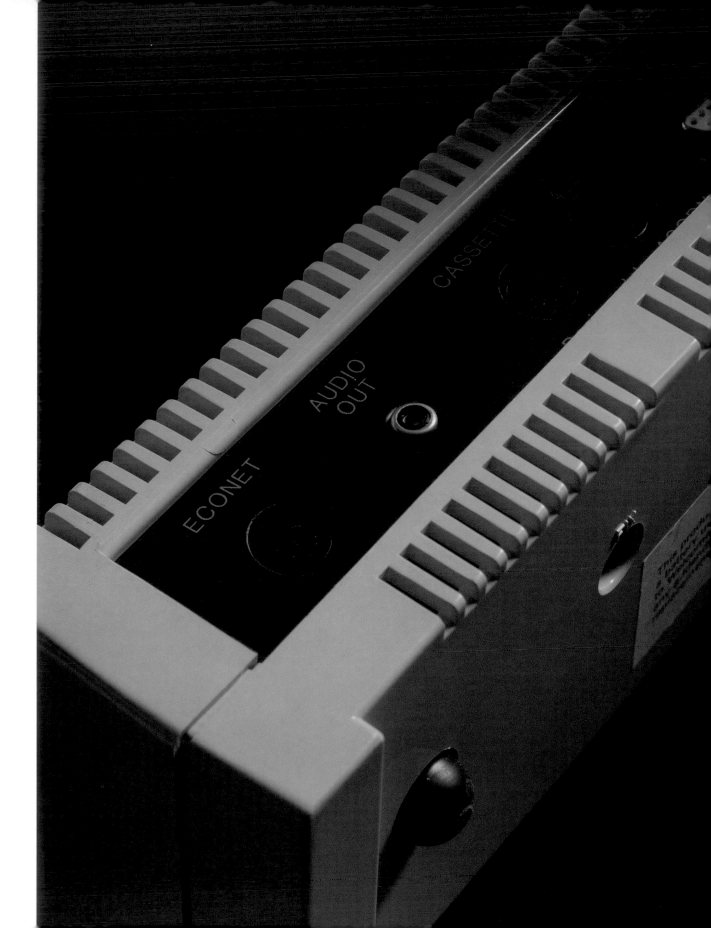

The mid-1980s were tumultuous for Acorn. It struggled to launch the Electron P.141 while taking the company public and making a failed attempt to set up a US subsidiary. And then, in 1984, the bottom fell out of the home computer market. In 1985 Olivetti P.224 bought a 49 per cent stake in Acorn, and it later took a controlling stake. And all the while, Acorn was working on two ambitious new projects. One was the BBC Master, an updated BBC Micro P.72 with an expanded keyboard and a ROM packed with the well-regarded View word processor and ViewSheet spreadsheet. It was a natural step forward for a system that had become standard in schools and universities, and it was quickly adopted. The other project was rather more future-facing P.213.

The Master's great asset was its extensibility: when fitted with a 4-MHz 65C102 coprocessor card, it would transform into the Master Turbo. When also fitted with a SCSI interface, a Videodisc Filing System ROM, a Philips VP415 Domesday Player coprocessor, and a trackball, it became the Master AIV, and was ready to take its part in the BBC Domesday Project. To mark the 900th anniversary of the first census of England, the BBC asked a million schoolchildren from over 9,000 British schools to record impressions of their local areas and daily lives. The aim was to produce a 'portrait in data and pictures of Britain', stored on two 300-MB LaserDiscs controlled by the Master AIV.

The Community Disc was navigated by a map and featured the children's work in text and photographs. The National Disc featured 1981 census data, video, and 'virtual walks', navigated as if walking around a gallery. The project was ambitious, but it's hard to say that it lived up to the predecessor it was designed to celebrate. While the original Domesday Book was inscribed on long-lasting vellum, the BBC's was on LaserDisc – soon superseded by new, higher-capacity formats – and navigated with a computer that its creators knew would only be in common use for a few short years.

ACORN
BBC MASTER 128

ACORN ARCHIMEDES A440

ORIGIN
United Kingdom

TECHNICAL DATA
ARM2 at 8 MHz, 4 MB RAM

AVAILABLE
July 1987

MANUFACTURER
Acorn Computers

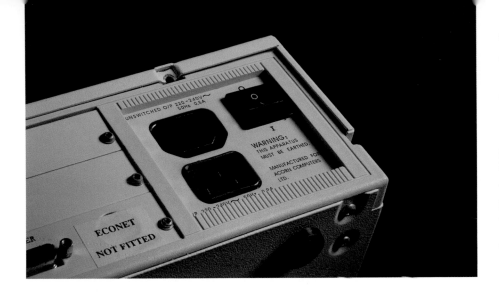

The Acorn Archimedes was the first RISC-based microcomputer, with a microprocessor that would define the future of computing. But it emerged from a problem very much of its own time. By 1983, the trusty 6502 microprocessor P.34 was ageing. Computer manufacturers began to look towards a new generation of chips, particularly 16-bit microprocessors such as the Motorola 68000, but Acorn looked another way. It saw a chance to design much faster computers with the faster memory that was coming on to the market. The trouble was, no microprocessor supported enough data bandwidth to take advantage of it.

Acorn cofounder Hermann Hauser had heard of IBM's 'reduced instruction set computing' (RISC), a principle by which a chip might run faster by using lots of simple instructions rather than fewer complex ones. Perhaps Acorn could design and make its own RISC processor? As hardware designers Sophie Wilson and Steve Furber set out on a tour of chip manufacturers, they visited National Semiconductor's vast Israel factory and assumed the task was beyond their resources. Then, in October 1983, they visited 6502 co-designer Bill Mensch at the Western Design Center in Arizona; Furber later described him as working with a small team on the Apple IIs P.31 in a suburban bungalow. They returned energized. Their little Cambridge company might pull it off.

Wilson architected a 32-bit chip and Furber prepared it for fabrication, discovering that RISC's simple instructions naturally led to a simple design. In April 1985, to their surprise, the first test chips immediately worked. The puzzle, though, was that Furber's multimeter couldn't detect them drawing current. By complete accident, the chip – known as the ARM – was extraordinarily power-efficient. Its first use was as a £4,500 add-on for the BBC Micro P.72, but its real debut, upgraded as the ARM2, was in a new Acorn range called the Archimedes. The ARM2's tiny power draw meant that it didn't need fans, and it had just 30,000 transistors compared to the 68000's 40,000. Yet, as game designer David Braben discovered while making *Lander*, a 3D game demo that shipped with the first model, it was incredibly fast. But this was just the start of the ARM's long and transformative history P.248.

MANUFACTURER
Cambridge Computer

AVAILABLE
August 1987

TECHNICAL DATA
Z80A at 3.3 MHz, 32 KB RAM

ORIGIN
United Kingdom

Clive Sinclair took one last stab at designing computers after he sold Sinclair Research's entire computer business to Amstrad in 1986 P. 207. He formed yet another new company, calling it Cambridge Computer, and went to work on the Z88, a portable computer that was years ahead of its time. Designed very specifically for computing on the move, it was small (it fitted on aeroplane tray tables) and light, at just 900 g (2 lb). It ran on four AA batteries, which gave it up to four hours of use, and automatically went into a battery-saving sleep mode after a few minutes of inactivity.

It was also a capable office machine. Its rubber keyboard was full-size; its 640-by-64-pixel LCD display was able to show up to 104 characters along 8 lines on the left and a 256-by-64-pixel graphical area on the right; and its software wasn't bad, either. The Z88's proprietary OZ operating system featured task-switching: if the user went to the Index, they could return to the document on which they were working, or any other program that was running, by selecting it from a Suspended Activities list. And the Z88 shipped with PipeDream, a combination of word processor and spreadsheet; full BBC BASIC; a diary; and 'popdowns', a series of overlaid tools including a calendar and calculator.

It was expandable, too. Three easily accessible bays under the keyboard held cartridges that could each expand the RAM by 128 KB and store data on EPROM cards. And, since its creators knew that the Z88 would most often be used as a second computer, its PC Link serial interface could convert its proprietary documents into the Wordstar and Lotus 1-2-3 standards of the time and send them to other computer formats.

In many ways the Z88 was the culmination of all Sinclair's design philosophies: small, cheap – its base model cost £300 – and future-gazing. Designed by Rick Dickinson, who had led on the ZX81, Spectrum, and beyond, the Z88, alongside Psion's Organiser II, was a blueprint for the forthcoming PDA. But Cambridge Computer wouldn't make another, instead moving into the world of satellite television receivers until it was sold off in 1990.

CAMBRIDGE Z88

Cambridge Z88, ROM cards ↑

ORIGIN
United Kingdom

TECHNICAL DATA
NEC V30 at 8 MHz, 512 KB RAM

AVAILABLE
March 1988

MANUFACTURER
Amstrad

AMSTRAD PPC 512

By the late 1980s, portability was a strong selling point for new IBM-compatible computers, and Amstrad, flush with the success of its PC range P. 207 was in just the right position to exploit it. Neither the PPC 512 nor the upgraded PPC 640 shared the portable elegance of the Z88 P. 215 that Clive Sinclair had launched the previous year. But they did, like all Amstrad's computers, have enough features to make them practical.

When closed, the PPC 512 could be carried with the handle on one end, and its full-size 102-key keyboard opened out on a hinge. It could run on ten replaceable batteries if there was no power source to plug into (but only for an hour); a car cigarette lighter; or an Amstrad monitor fitted with a power supply, such as the PC-CD model that came with the PC series. It came supplied with MS-DOS 3.3 and PPC Organizer, a suite of software that included a word processor, calendar, and contacts book 'for the executive on the move', and alongside the 640 KB of RAM in the PPC 640 it also included a modem.

The PPC computers were let down by their small fold-out monochrome LCD screens, which displayed forty or eighty characters (depending on graphics mode) on each of their twenty-five lines, but at such low contrast that many found them hard to make out. The PPCs also weighed a hefty 5 kg (11 lb) each. But, as ever, Amstrad had produced the cheapest portable PCs on the market. They sported the NEC V30 microprocessor, a reverse-engineered Intel 8088 that tended to perform faster at the same clock speeds and featured the same pin layout as an 8086. Such judicious cost-saving meant that the base PPC 512 launched at £460. The two computers didn't sell on the scale of Amstrad's desktops, but the company knew that portable was the future. Laptops remained an important part of its computing business until 1997, when it closed. Amstrad wasn't an inventive company, or one that tended to raise passion, but it played a profound role in pushing the computer into European homes.

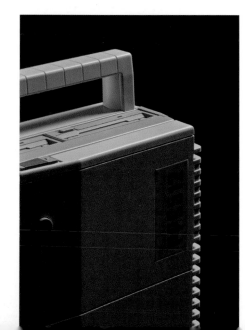

Amstrad PPC 512, carry handle ↑

MANUFACTURER
Sinclair Research

AVAILABLE
November 1988

TECHNICAL DATA
Intel 8086 at 8 MHz, 512 KB RAM

ORIGIN
United Kingdom

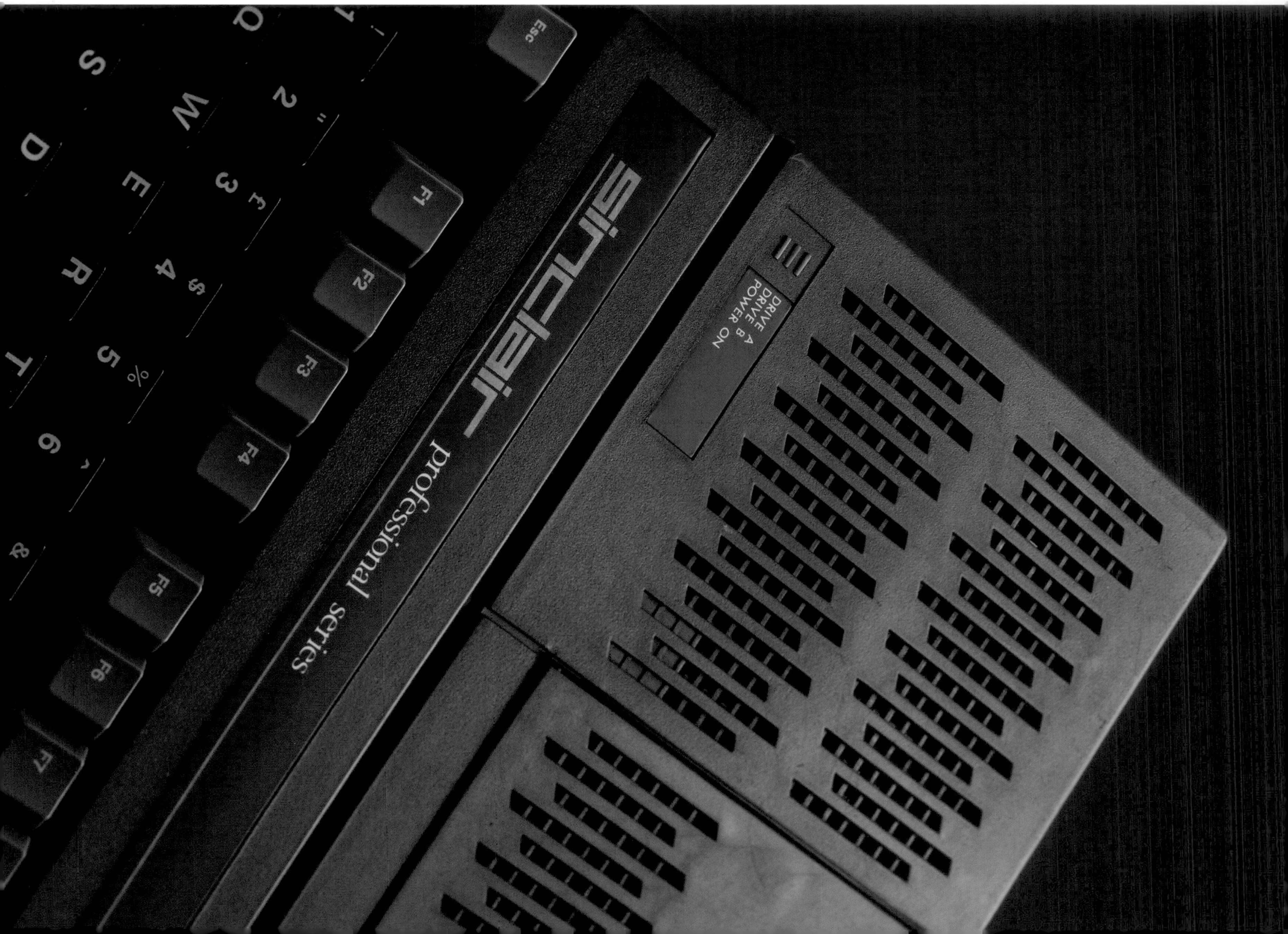

sinclair

professional series

DRIVE A
DRIVE B
POWER ON

Esc

F1
F2
F3
F4
F5
F6
F7

!
1
"
2
£
3
$
4
%
5
`
6
&

Q
W
E
R
T

S

D

Sinclair's last computers weren't Sinclairs. The PC 500 was a rebadged PC 1512 P. 207, and the PC 200 was a refactored PPC P. 216, its folding case exchanged for a black one with an integrated keyboard and its screen removed in favour of a TV-out. If you lived in the US, you wouldn't even know it as a Sinclair: its case was tan, and it was badged as an Amstrad PC 20. By 1988, two years after buying Sinclair Research's computing assets, Amstrad had wrung out almost all it was going to get from the Spectrum P. 170, having launched its final model, the +3, the previous year.

The PC 200 was an attempt to wrest just a little more out of the brand, and to present a cheap PC to the family market for which Sinclair had made computers since the ZX80. But Amstrad had already lost it to the 520 ST P. 191 and Amiga P. 195. Apparently, the company believed that the PPC's 16-bit microprocessor could play up to their standards. It couldn't.

'Is it a Spectrum? Is it an ST? No, it's a disappointment,' reported UK gaming magazine *Crash!*. The PC 200 didn't support any true Sinclair software, and with CGA graphics that only allowed four colours, the PC 200 utterly lacked the colourful punch of the 16-bit home computers. It didn't even live up to EGA, the newer PC standard, which supported sixteen colours. Besides, Amstrad had established a booming PC range of its own, which easily eclipsed any business appeal the PC 200 might have had. And if you wanted a multi-use (by which you probably meant gaming) machine, you would get an Amiga. The PC 200's £299 launch price was low enough, but being up against so many better options, Amstrad only marketed it for a few months before quietly making it disappear. The PC 500 met an even more obscure fate. And that, for Sinclair's name in computing, was that.

SINCLAIR PC 200

MANUFACTURER
NeXT

AVAILABLE
October 1988

TECHNICAL DATA
Motorola 68030 at 25 MHz,
4 MB–16 MB RAM

ORIGIN
United States

NEXT
COMPUTER

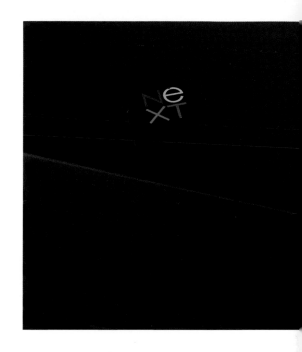

Steve Jobs left Apple only a few months after fellow-founder Steve Wozniak. Apple's CEO, John Sculley, had reorganized Jobs away from his beloved Macintosh P. 151, believing that Apple's future lay in avoiding trying to compete with the PC by building computers like the Apple II P. 203 for small businesses and homes. Jobs believed that Apple's future was in powerful, closed-architecture computers such as the Macintosh, but he had been made powerless as head of New Product Development – whatever that meant. In September 1985, following a series of tussles with Sculley for control of Apple, Jobs resigned and, taking several executives with him, founded a new company called NeXT.

NeXT was anxious not to compete with Apple, and the initial idea was to make workstations for higher education that could perform complex scientific analysis and simulations, while also being cheap enough for students to use. But that soon changed. Jobs wanted to make software, too, hiring Avie Tevanian to lead a team to design the next generation of the graphical user interface that the Lisa P. 146 and Macintosh had pioneered. Called NeXTSTEP, it was based on a UNIX core and was the first operating system to implement the object-oriented programming paradigm, which gave powerful control over how data could interact with other data. It also developed and polished many other features that are taken for granted today, such as a permanent dock that gave constant easy access to applications; dragging and dropping text, images, and other media between different applications; large icons; enhanced typography; and a 3D look. And it was all contained within a foot-long black magnesium cube fashioned by Frog Design, with a $100,000 logo designed by graphic designer Paul Rand.

The NeXT Computer was the finest expression yet of Jobs's uncompromising melding of hardware, software, and visual design, and it naturally came at a cost. A price tag of $6,500 meant that it competed with neither Apple nor IBM, but its legacy is incontrovertible. It was used by Tim Berners-Lee to write WorldWideWeb, the first web browser, and the first web server software, and by id Software to create the game *Doom*. In 1990, NeXT released a new version, the NeXTcube, but it wasn't until NeXTSTEP was converted to run on Intel processors in 1993 that the company finally turned a profit.

MANUFACTURER
SMT Goupil

AVAILABLE
1988

TECHNICAL DATA
Intel 80286 at 10 MHz, 640 KB RAM

ORIGIN
France

Goupil weathered the storms of the 1980s only slightly better than other French computer manufacturers. With a focus on corporate and administrative clients and on hard-edged industrial design, usually in black, in 1985 Goupil claimed it held 15 per cent of the French market, despite also being in significant debt. Five years later, unlike Matra Hachette P. 197 and Thomson P. 199, it held 18 per cent of the market with a tenacity that was partly down to its early adoption of the IBM-compatible PC. But, while that strategy meant it avoided the price wars roiling in the cheap end of the market, by the end of the 1980s Goupil was facing new competitors.

The Golf was a portable office computer, which Goupil marketed as having 'power, mobility and style'. Powered initially by a 80286 running at 10 MHz, and later with a slightly faster 12-MHz microprocessor alongside a more powerful 80386 model, it was power enough. And its slim body was very portable, since it weighed only 3.7 kg (8 lb), although it didn't have a battery.

But it was the Golf's picture frame-like screen, which contained a 640-by-480-pixel black-and-white LCD display, that was its most eye-catching feature. It was possible to separate it from the main body of the computer and to prop it up using a folding stand. Goupil boasted of wide viewing angles and a bright backlight, and its tones could also be reversed for maximum readability, athough many complained it was so unresponsive that they couldn't see a moving mouse pointer.

All these premium features came with a premium price, of course, and the Golf didn't sell many units. American PC manufacturers such as Compaq, Gateway, and Dell P. 221 were sweeping through the market, selling far cheaper machines with far less style but often more power, while drastic cuts in French government spending knocked out Goupil's traditional market. Goupil would go on to release only one more desktop computer before it was finally liquidated in 1991.

GOUPIL GOLF 286

ORIGIN
Italy

TECHNICAL DATA
NEC V40 at 8 MHz, 512 KB RAM

AVAILABLE
May 1988

MANUFACTURER
Olivetti

Not to be confused with the Olivetti Prodest PC128 (which was a rebadged Thomson MO6 P. 199), or the Prodest PC128s (which was a rebadged BBC Master Compact P. 211), the Prodest PC 1 was an XT-based PC that was intended to compete with the reasonably popular Schneider Euro PC. It didn't sell very well.

Olivetti had a long history as a computer maker. It had pioneered transistor-based mainframes with the likes of the Elea 9000 in 1957, and commercial, desktop-scale calculator-computers with the remarkably stylish Programma 101, which was based on a design worked on by Z80 designer Federico Faggin, in 1965. But having missed out on the emergence of the home computer in the 1970s, Olivetti was largely commissioning machines based on other systems and industrial design, such as the 1983 M10 laptop, which was a repurposed Kyotronic KC-85 (itself a trailblazing portable computer released in the US by Tandy as the TRS-80 Model 100). In the mid-1980s Olivetti had bought a controlling share of Acorn Computers and was a partner of French manufacturer Thomson: hence the provenance of the Prodest family. But despite these holdings, from 1989 Olivetti became purely a maker of PCs.

Schneider, the maker of the Euro PC, had previously rebadged Amstrad computers and sold them on the German market. It had watched the rise of the PC as closely as Amstrad, moving to make its own low-power but slimline and cheap PC just as Amstrad launched the functionally identical Sinclair 200 P. 219. Between them, they did a great deal to introduce Europe to the IBM-compatible computer, with Schneider releasing several in the Euro PC line alongside a series of more standard desktops. The PC had taken over Europe.

OLIVETTI PRODEST PC1

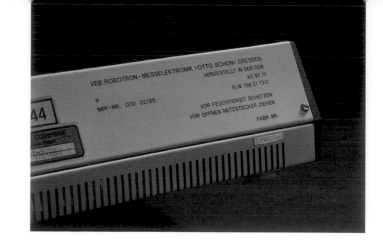

ORIGIN
German Democratic Republic

TECHNICAL DATA
MME U880 at 2.5 MHz, 16 KB RAM

AVAILABLE
1986

MANUFACTURER
VEB Robotron-Messelektronik

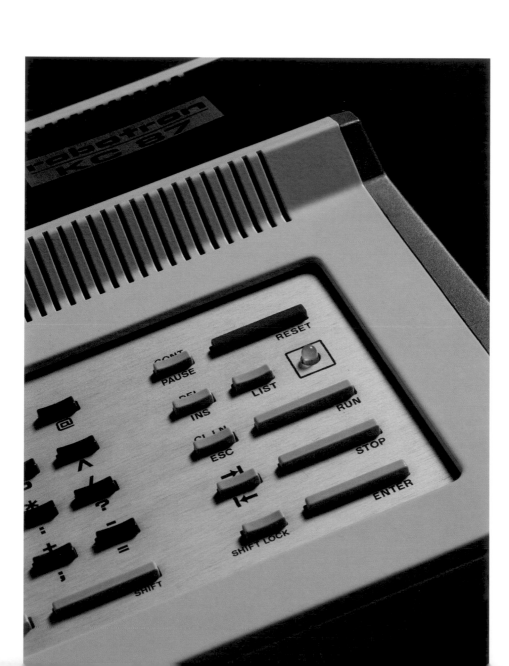

ROBOTRON KC 87

Computers were very hard to come by in the East Germany of the 1980s. Few Western machines made their way through the checkpoints that divided Germany, because they had been embargoed. Western states had agreed not to export them to any of the countries of the Eastern Bloc, partly for fear of them being used for military purposes. Even domestically produced computers, such as the Robotron KC 87, only rarely made their way into homes.

The KC 87 was one in a series of 8-bit computers produced by Robotron. It was largely identical to the first model, the Z 9001, which launched in 1984, and the rebadged KC 85/1; each came as either colour or monochrome. The KC 87, however, featured built-in BASIC. The range's U880 microprocessor was an unlicensed clone of the Z80 with a few minor changes, and was the most commonly used CPU in East Germany and the most advanced in the Eastern Bloc, since most other countries only produced 8080 clones.

Rather than homes, computers in East Germany were most commonly found in schools, universities, businesses, and other organizations. But computer clubs still formed; there were twenty of them in Berlin by 1988. Many clubs, however, disdained the likes of the KC 87, not least for its terrible keyboard. Membership of the most exclusive clubs was down to ownership of computers such as the Commodore 64, which was made only a few hundred miles away in West Germany. The clubs were quite aware that the Stasi, East Germany's secret police, was taking a keen interest in their activities. Informants passed on intelligence about which computers were owned by which clubs, along with membership lists, with agents noting that they often included people with 'a verifiably negative attitude toward the socialist state and social order'. The Stasi was also worried that software from the West might hold viruses that damaged state holdings. Most clubs, of course, simply exchanged games such as *The Last Ninja*, *Frogger*, and *Raid Over Moscow*, which the Stasi noted as having 'a particularly militaristic and inhuman nature'.

ORIGIN
Ukraine

TECHNICAL DATA
Goldstar Z80A at 3.5 MHz, 64 KB RAM

AVAILABLE
1989

MANUFACTURER
Dnepropetrovsk Machine-Building Plant

The Orel BK-08 wasn't the only ZX Spectrum P. 91 clone made in the Soviet Union. There were the Baltica, Hobbit, Krasnogorsk, Best III, Composite, GrandRomMax, Didaktik M P. 230, Leningrad, Delta, and many others: more Spectrum clones were made in the Soviet Union than any other part of the world. The Spectrum was, after all, exceedingly hard to get hold of there, because computer exports to the Soviet Bloc were tightly controlled. But after the Micro-80 kit design was published in a popular electronics magazine called *Radio* in 1978, a strong appetite for microcomputers had begun to grow, despite the government deciding not to invest in doing its own research into computing technology. So a market for knockoff machines developed, safe from any danger of legal problems.

The BK-08 was manufactured in the Dnepropetrovsk Machine-Building Plant, a factory in Ukraine where ballistic missiles were also made, between around 1989 and 1995. Almost every component was made in the Soviet Bloc; while early units featured a Z80 made by East German manufacturer MME, later units used one made by Goldstar in Korea. The BK-08's ROM supported Cyrillic characters, and it shipped with MZ80, a full-featured machine code monitor.

Indeed, while the BK-08 is described as a clone of the Spectrum, it wasn't a straight copy. It had more RAM, and it didn't force wait cycles while accessing RAM, making it run quicker than a standard machine. It also featured shadow RAM, a tool that programmers could use to test code and even write new ROMs: if they moved a program to a special 16-KB part of the memory that was not flushed when the computer was reset, the BK-08 would then attempt to boot from it. They were useful tweaks, but they also meant that the BK-08 only had partial compatibility for the floods of pirated games that came through the Iron Curtain.

OREL BK-08

ORIGIN
Czechoslovakia

TECHNICAL DATA
Z80A at 4 MHz, 48 KB RAM

AVAILABLE
1990

MANUFACTURER
Didaktik Skalica

Alongside the Orel BK-08 P. 228 and the many Spectrum clones made in the Soviet Union came those made by Didaktik Skalica, an electronics company based in Bratislava in former Czechoslovakia. Its first two computers, the Alfa and Beta, were based on the Intel 8080 and built for schools, but Didaktik soon realized it could enjoy much bigger returns if it leaned on the Spectrum's huge software library and widely documented hardware.

Its first Spectrum clone was the Gama, which was released in 1987 and somehow featured the Spectrum's Ferranti ULA chip, so it was widely compatible with its original. The M, released in 1990, wasn't so close a clone. In place of the original Spectrum's custom ULA was the T34B1 chip made by Angstrem, a major Russian producer of integrated circuits, and this change led to its video output being square rather than using the original's screen-filling 4:3 ratio. Other changes moved the Didaktik M further away from the original Spectrum design and towards an informal new Soviet standard that included Cyrillic language support and fixes to bugs in the original hardware and ROM.

Inside, the M had 64 KB of RAM, only 48 KB of which was available to use, and a peculiarly unfriendly interface connector that wasn't compatible with any devices available in the Soviet Union, forcing users to rig up their own solutions. Its keyboard, meanwhile, was roundly criticized for its low quality, with badly set keys that were difficult to press accurately. It was succeeded in 1992 by the Kompakt, which was identical to the M but for a 3.5-in. disk drive built into its right side. But it wasn't actually made by Didaktik: having moved on to manufacture PCs, it had sold the design to a one-man company called Kompakt Servis. Still, the popularity of these machines meant that Spectrum format software continued to be published by companies such as Ultrasoft and Proxima well into the 1990s, as Czechoslovakia dissolved and the Czech Republic and Slovakia formed. Proxima also published *ZX Magazine*, the key rag for the beloved '*gumák*', a nickname for the M that was based on the Czech word for rubber and inspired by the original's keyboard.

DIDAKTIK M

ORIGIN
United Kingdom

TECHNICAL DATA
Zilog Z80B at 6 MHz, 256 KB or
512 KB RAM

MGT SAM COUPÉ

AVAILABLE
December 1989

MANUFACTURER
Miles Gordon Technology

It's easy to smirk at the idea of an 8-bit computer being released in the age of 16-bit, but the idea behind the Z80-powered SAM Coupé was to build a cheap and natural upgrade to the star of the previous generation, the ZX Spectrum P. 91. Its maker, Miles Gordon Technology (MGT), was definitely part of the family. Founders Alan Miles and Bruce Gordon had worked at Sinclair Research before they founded MGT in 1986 to make clever interfaces such as the DISCiPLE, which allowed owners to connect floppy drives to their Spectrums and control them with simple commands. But they knew times were changing, and their long-term plan was for MGT to build a computer of its own.

Under its fancy name and distinctive casing, the SAM Coupé was able to run a graphics mode identical to the Spectrum's, even if its processor was rated at twice the speed. It also had more RAM and new sound hardware. But the way it shared RAM between video and CPU meant it only operated a little faster than the Spectrum when running native programs, such as the bundled art application Flash!. If you wanted to play Spectrum games, you needed to load a copy of its ROM (for copyright reasons, MGT couldn't supply it), and the Coupé didn't support Spectrum 128K P. 170 software.

The Coupé came with some modern benefits, such as SAM BASIC, which featured many advanced commands, including those for drawing sprites and vectors. But as something of a ship stranded between two ports, it didn't sell well: MGT ended up with a lot of unsold stock, and went into receivership in 1990. But it wasn't quite the end. Miles and Gordon bought its assets and formed SAM Computers to sell the Coupé, with floppy drive, at under £200. They also released new peripherals and software, and they survived another couple of years before folding. And still the Coupé lived on: the stock was next bought by West Coast Computers, who overhauled it to create the SAM Élite, with 512 KB of RAM. Against the odds, a committed base of developers and users grew as the Coupé lived its tangled life, but estimates suggest it only sold 12,000 units.

MGT SAM Coupé, underside, detail ↑

ORIGIN
United Kingdom

TECHNICAL DATA
Zilog Z80A at 4 MHz, 64 KB RAM

AVAILABLE
September 1990

MANUFACTURER
Amstrad

Six years was a long time during the home computer gold rush. Between 1984 and 1990, hardware evolved from one generation into the next. Amstrad thought that it could stick a finger in the dyke by updating its venerable and hugely popular CPC 464 P. 157 and 6128 P. 173, largely focusing on form factor. It threw their aged components into a case that looked like an Amiga P. 195 or ST P. 191, only upgrading a few details – including adding a cartridge slot, hardware scrolling and support for sixteen sprites, programmable interrupts, and 15 colours from a palette of 4,096 – and removed the 'CPC' from their name.

But while they occupied the very pinnacle of *their* generation, the 464plus and 6128plus couldn't compete with the prevailing one, in which computers happily threw around 256 colours and all the sprites a programmer could want. The Plus computers were resolutely old, and low sales led to Amstrad withdrawing them from sale in 1992.

Alongside the Plus range, Amstrad also released the GX4000, a game console built on the 464plus hardware and costing £99.99, with £25 games. It aimed to compete with Nintendo and Sega, but against the rich colour and sound of Sega's Mega Drive (which was launched at around the same time in Europe) and with slow support from game publishers, it faced a similar fate to the Plus range. And Amstrad hadn't quite finished building awkward amalgams of computers and consoles. In 1993 it released the Amstrad Mega PC, which somehow bolted a Mega Drive into an 80386-powered PC. It sold badly at a launch price of £999, which was later reduced to £599. While this chain of failures was unspooling, Amstrad was growing apart from computers. Its focus had shifted to telecommunications, particularly building set-top boxes for Sky, the UK's leading satellite TV provider. After having made a fortune from home computers, it saw opportunities for making a new one elsewhere.

AMSTRAD 464PLUS

ORIGIN
United States

TECHNICAL DATA
Intel 80C88 at 4.9 MHz, 128 KB RAM

AVAILABLE
June 1989

MANUFACTURER
Atari Corporation

Even though its ST P. 191 lagged behind Commodore's Amiga P. 195, Atari was breaking its own sales records at the end of the 1980s and still had the ambition to be a technological leader, particularly in the fast-emerging world of portable computers. In September 1989 it released the Lynx, a handheld colour console that easily outperformed Nintendo's Game Boy in raw power, if not sales, and in June of the same year it had released the first 'palmtop' computer, the Atari Portfolio.

Ostensibly a PC weighing just 500 g (1 lb) and measuring 20 cm (7⅞ in.) wide, 10.5 cm (4⅛ in.) deep, and 2.5 cm (1 in.) high, the Portfolio was a true handheld computer. But it wasn't actually designed by Atari. It was created by a UK-based company called DIP Research, which was founded by three former Psion employees. Psion had specialized in handheld computers since it launched the Organiser in 1984; DIP was set on taking the same direction and licensed its first computer to Atari to sell in both the UK and the US, where it cost $499.95 at launch.

The Portfolio came with surprisingly few compromises. Its unlit LCD display wasn't great and could only display forty characters on each of its eight lines, but it ran on three AA batteries, which could last a remarkable 100 hours of use, and it could hold data in its memory while they were being changed. And while the Portfolio's size didn't make for comfortable typing, its tiny keys were useable.

Its main compromise was its software. Rather than MS-DOS, it ran DIP-DOS, a proprietary operating system that was mostly compatible with the rather elderly MS-DOS 2.11. It meant that most more sophisticated PC software didn't work with the Portfolio, but it did come with a suite of Lotus 1-2-3 office applications, a contacts book, and a scheduler. The hope was that the Portfolio's size and always-available convenience would be its reason for existence, but it was probably a little too pioneering for its own good. John Connor in *Terminator 2* saw its potential, though – he used it to hack into an ATM.

ATARI PORTFOLIO

ORIGIN
United States

TECHNICAL DATA
68000 at 8 MHz, 2 MB RAM

AVAILABLE
September 1989

MANUFACTURER
Atari Corporation

ATARI STACY2

Atari didn't stop exploring portable computers in 1989 with the handheld Portfolio P.236. A few months later it launched a laptop version of its 1040 ST, complete with a 3.5-in. disk drive, a trackball, and a monochrome 640-by-400-pixel backlit LCD screen. However, quite unlike the Portfolio, the STacy was only really portable in name. For a start, it weighed 7 kg (15½ lb), but more importantly, it didn't ship with any batteries. The space under the screen, to the right of its hinge, was meant to be filled with twelve of them, but Atari discovered at the end of its development that the STacy was so power-hungry that they would only power it for a few minutes before being exhausted. To avoid public uproar, at the last minute Atari stripped out the internal contacts, sealed the hatch, and left the space empty.

Only 35,000 units were ever sold. The base machine, after all, cost an eye-watering $2,299 at launch. But at that price the STacy was a modest success; Atari CEO Jack Tramiel had only forecast the need to make 5,000 a month, and it easily undercut the price of Apple's Macintosh Portable P.240. Furthermore, the STacy's MIDI ports made it appealing to the music industry: the band Duran Duran used one to sequence tracks, and it was also used to complete production on the music for the movie *Born on the Fourth of July*. Although Tramiel always had an eye for making computers inexpensive, the STacy was most definitely a professional machine; the STacy2 and STacy4, which released at the same time, featured 2 MB and 4 MB of RAM respectively and were supplied with hard drives.

Atari had another go at a portable ST with the altogether more elegant ST BOOK in 1991. It was quiet, light, and ran for hours on its battery, due in part to the fact that its screen wasn't backlit. Elegance was never a surefire route to success in the computer industry, however. Atari never released the ST BOOK in the US, and it only sold 1,000 units in Europe.

Atari STacy2, integral trackball ↑

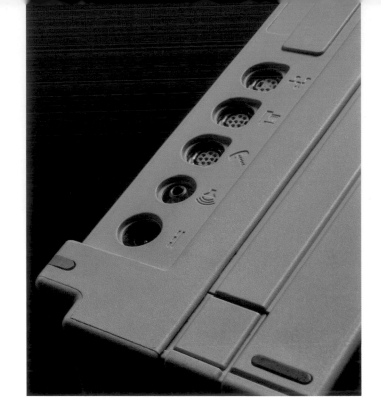

ORIGIN
United States

TECHNICAL DATA
Motorola 68HC000 at 16 MHz, 1 MB RAM

AVAILABLE
September 1989

MANUFACTURER
Apple Computer

APPLE MACINTOSH PORTABLE

In developing the Macintosh `P.151` Apple had acquired a knack for design-ing self-contained computers, but the Portable was its first 'luggable' one. Complete with an internal battery and integrated screen, it was huge, heavy, and very expensive. In itself the Macintosh Portable was not a great success, but it provided the foundation for a line of computers that would come to define Apple in the years ahead.

At 7 kg (15½ lb), the Portable wasn't the heaviest luggable around – the Philips P2000C `P.144` was twice that – but at 10 cm (3⅞ in.) thick, it wouldn't fit on an airliner's tray table. Most of its weight was down to its lead-acid battery. This was a monster that could power the Portable for up to ten hours, but it came with a few caveats besides its sheer size. Its life was significantly shortened if it was fully drained, and if it had no charge the computer couldn't run off AC power because of a quirk in the way it was wired together. All in all, the Macintosh Portable placed quite a burden of power management on its owner.

Worse, the Portable, which cost $7,300 with a hard drive, was meant to offer the full performance of a desktop in a portable format, but it was launched right alongside the rather more powerful Macintosh IIci, which ran on the

68030 microprocessor. That's not to say the Portable was underpowered – it had more juice than the desktop Macintosh SE, which only launched a couple of years earlier – but the contrast did it few favours.

In early 1991, low sales led Apple to release a cheaper model with a backlit screen that improved readability, and also with slower and more power-hungry memory. These changes saw the Portable's battery life halved, but only a few months later, in October 1991, Apple made the Portable obsolete when it launched the PowerBook 100 series. Its bottom-rung entry, the PowerBook 100, had the same fundamental specifications as the Portable, but it was a third of the price, a third of the weight, and sported an elegant book-like design by Apple Industrial Design Group. While the Portable struggled to find an audience, the PowerBook exploded. With it, the age of the laptop truly began.

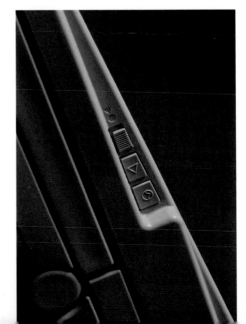

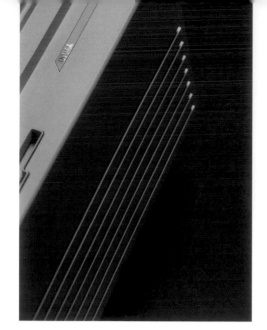

A somewhat souped-up ST, the TT030 was first formulated all the way back in 1986 as a Unix-based workstation capable of competing with Apple's Macintosh II, which came out in 1987. But it wasn't released until 1990, a victim of its own tortuous development as Atari tried to keep up with the latest microprocessor standards. It was first based on Motorola's 68020, a new version of the 520 ST's chip P. 191 that supported full 32-bit instructions. But as it was designed, the 68030 was released, giving even better 32-bit features and a 32-MHz clock speed, and Atari decided to switch.

The need to maintain compatibility with the ST complicated matters, however: it meant that the computer had to use the same video and sound chips. Since they didn't support the 68030's speedy new standards, the TT030 had to adopt a Frankenstein-style architecture that ran the processor and system bus at different clock speeds. Still, the TT030 was powerful for the time, albeit at a workstation price of $2,995 on its US release in 1991.

The other problem was Unix. For the first two years of its life, the TT030 shipped with version 3.01 of TOS, the operating system that came with the original 520 ST. But it was meant to be used with Unix, a powerful operating system that was first developed at Bell Labs in the early 1970s before spreading into universities, where it expanded to include multitasking capabilities and many other functions. Unix quickly became the bedrock for network design and the formation of the Internet as it propagated outside academia in the 1980s, and so it was an attractive feature for computer users.

Atari had written a version of Unix long before the TT030 was released, but when Unix System V Release 4 was announced, Atari switched over to it. Just as changes to its microprocessor had complicated the TT030 itself, this late turnabout meant that the Atari System V wasn't released until 1992. By then, Commodore's Amiga Unix, based on the same standard, had already withered in the face of the PC's dominance, and Atari itself was about to return to a focus on videogames. The very final ST was the 1992 Falcon, but it was shelved after only a year on the market, and Atari's history as a home computer maker ended.

ATARI TT030

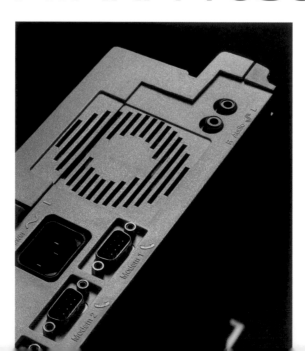

ORIGIN
United States

TECHNICAL DATA
Motorola 68030 at 32 MHz, 2 MB RAM

AVAILABLE
August 1990

MANUFACTURER
Atari Corporation

COMMODORE AMIGA A-500 PLUS

ORIGIN
United States

TECHNICAL DATA
Motorola 68000 at 7.1 MHz, 1 MB RAM

AVAILABLE
December 1991

MANUFACTURER
Commodore International

The release of the Amiga 500 in 1987 marked the point at which Commodore finally nailed down the Amiga's appeal: not as some highfalutin workstation (even if it was powerful enough to be one), but as a home computer and a true successor to the 64 P. 79. The Commodore 128 P. 188 lent the 500 its TV-friendly form factor, and it shipped with a more practical 512 KB of RAM at a fair price of $699. Its value steadily increased through price drops and software bundles that included games, such as *Batman*, which was temporarily exclusive to the bundle, and Deluxe Paint, the graphics editor that was used to create many of the Amiga's games.

In all, Commodore sold between four and five million 500s in Europe and North America. This didn't approach the incredible popularity of the 64, but it did make the 500 the leading home computer format of an age dominated by gaming consoles and IBM-compatibles. Commodore built on it in 1992 with the A-500 Plus. In fact, the A-500 Plus began to appear at the very end of 1991, sold as if it was a standard 500, apparently because Commodore had run out of stock to satisfy the Christmas rush. Its 1 MB of RAM was a bonus, but compatibility issues with its new versions of Kickstart, the Amiga's startup software, and Workbench, its GUI desktop, made some software unplayable without using a Kickstart switcher board or ReloKick software to roll back to Kickstart 1.3.

Designed to sustain the bottom of the range for a little longer, the Plus was cheaper to build than the standard 500, but it was discontinued just six months later in 1992 to make room for the miniaturized 600 and the 1200. Packing the beefier Motorola 68020 microprocessor and the Amiga Advanced Graphics Architecture, and costing $599, the 1200 represented the pinnacle of the Amiga as a home computer, but it couldn't prevent Commodore's fall.

The truth was that the Amiga never captured the same attention in North America as it did in Europe, and even Commodore's highest-specification Amigas, such as the 3000, lagged behind the power of the PC and Mac. Sound Blaster and VGA, meanwhile, had raised the PC's sound and graphics capabilities, making them more than equal to the Amiga's gaming prowess. In 1994, the company filed for bankruptcy.

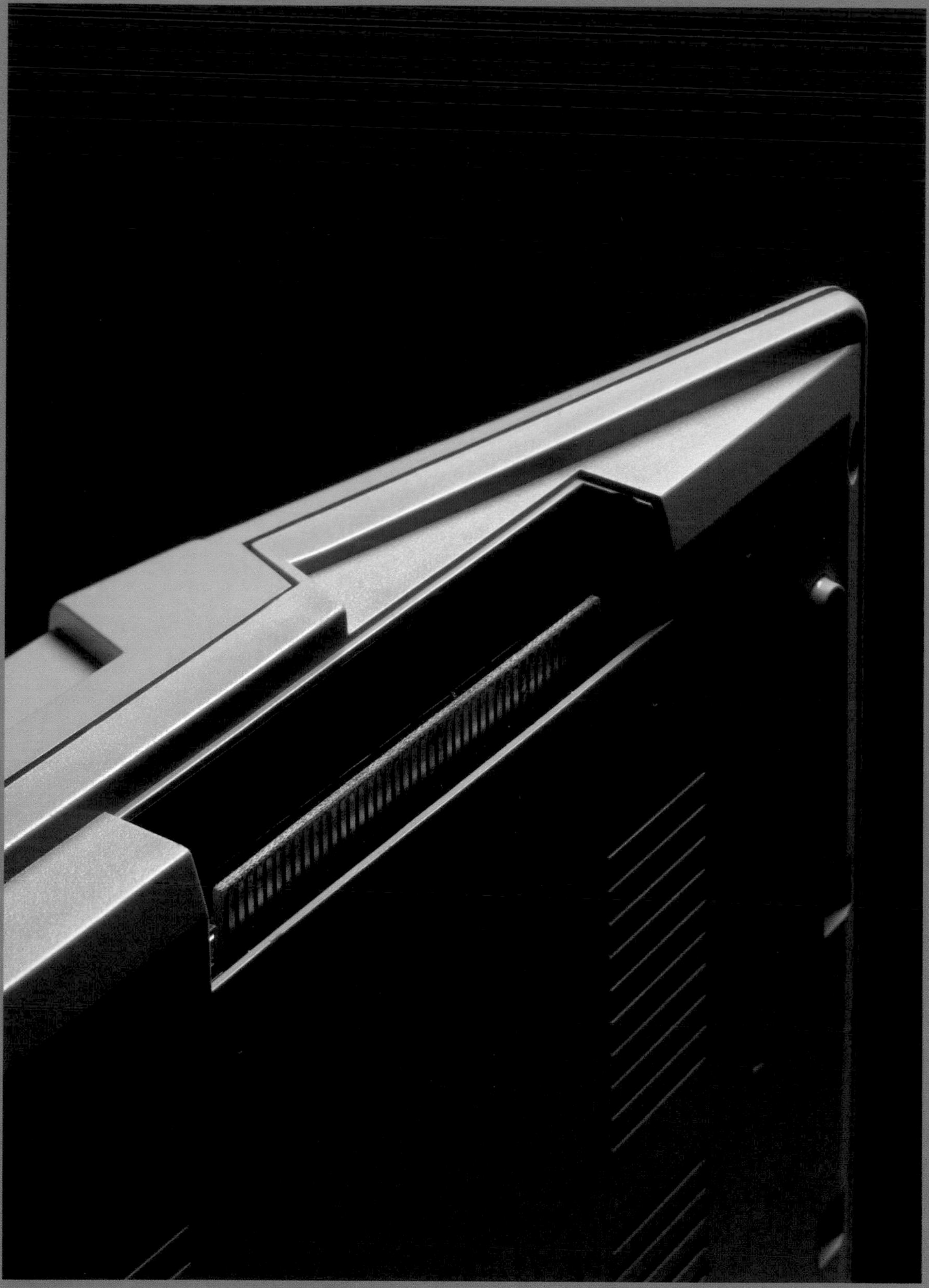

Commodore Amiga A-500 Plus, expansion port ↓

ORIGIN
United Kingdom

TECHNICAL DATA
ARM250 at 12 MHz, 1 MB or 2 MB RAM

AVAILABLE
September 1992

MANUFACTURER
Acorn Computers

Acorn's Archimedes range  P. 213 continued to grow throughout the late 1980s and into the 1990s. In 1989, the A3000 shipped with an upgrade of Acorn's Arthur operating system, now called RISC OS 2. OS 3 shipped with the A5000 in 1991, along with a new version of Acorn's microprocessor, the ARM3. The following year saw the release of the A3010, priced at £499. This was Acorn's family computer, fitted with joystick ports and TV-out, and designed to sit alongside the Amiga P. 244 and ST P. 191. Pricey and lacking their rich software collections, the A3010 didn't really compete with them, despite its ARM250 processor, which generally easily surpassed the power of every competitor.

In classic Acorn style, the A3010 was practical and future-minded. RISC OS 3.10 was a progressive graphical operating system with a desktop (the Pinboard), windows, a taskbar (the Icon Bar), and various useful applications, such as a text editor, drawing software, and a calculator. It didn't support 'true' multitasking – it instead featured cooperative multitasking, which gave processing time to whatever application was in the foreground – but it was as advanced an operating system as was available at the time, and it was all packed into a vast 1-MB ROM.

But Acorn's OS never made a dent in the leading operating systems, particularly Windows. The microprocessor inside the A3010, however, would go on to far greater things. The ARM250 was ARM's first System on a Chip (SoC). Rather than spreading all the necessary memory, input-output, and sound and video controllers across a motherboard on individual chips, everything came packed in a single one. The A3010 fundamentally *was* its microprocessor, and it established the line of SoC chips that powered the smartphone revolution to come, chiefly because of ARM's fabulously low power draw. Acorn had realized the importance of ARM, splitting it into its own company in 1990 so that Apple could use an ARM chip in its Newton personal digital assistant (PDA). ARM was still principally owned by Acorn, but this freedom allowed it to grow, and its chips became the most widely used 32-bit processors in the world.

ACORN A3010

DELL 316SX

ORIGIN
United States

TECHNICAL DATA
Intel 80386SX at 6 MHz, 512 KB RAM

AVAILABLE
1988

MANUFACTURER
Dell Computer Corporation

The thing about the PC was that it was built from off-the-shelf components. Anyone could design and market one, even a student. A student, say, studying at the University of Texas. A student, perhaps, called Michael Dell. Dell was fascinated by computers; when he got his first, an Apple II, he took it apart to see how it worked. In 1983, at the age of 19, he started his own business selling upgraded PCs and parts, and called it 'PC's Limited'. He advertised his first computer, the $795 Turbo PC, in computer magazines, offering custom options, and won bids to supply the State of Texas with hardware. Twelve months later, working from an apartment and having earned tens of thousands of dollars, his company had grossed $73 million.

Dell could see something that other PC makers couldn't. By selling computers directly to customers, rather than through shops, he could offer the lowest prices while understanding exactly what customers wanted and building PCs to fit. With these two simple principles, Dell built a company that could respond instantly to changing needs and new components as they came on to the market. The beige box wasn't as important as the ever-shifting bits inside it and the low price they cost. Other companies, such as Gateway, soon followed Dell's lead, greatly expanding the PC as a platform and leaving IBM far behind them.

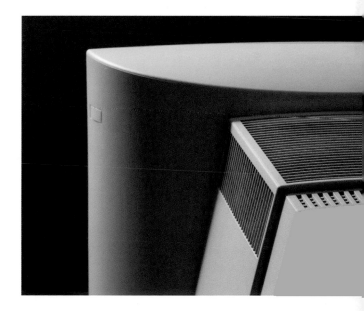

In 1987, as the company became large enough to go international, Dell renamed PC's Limited to Dell Computer Corporation and expanded into the UK. Throughout this period, Dell sold into businesses, and he wasn't interested in the consumer market. For him, entering the home computer market meant having to advertise more widely and suffering lower profit margins. But in 1996, with the growth of the Internet, that changed. By selling through its own website, Dell could cut out advertising and market its computers even more directly to customers. In 1997, the site was generating over $1 million in sales per day.

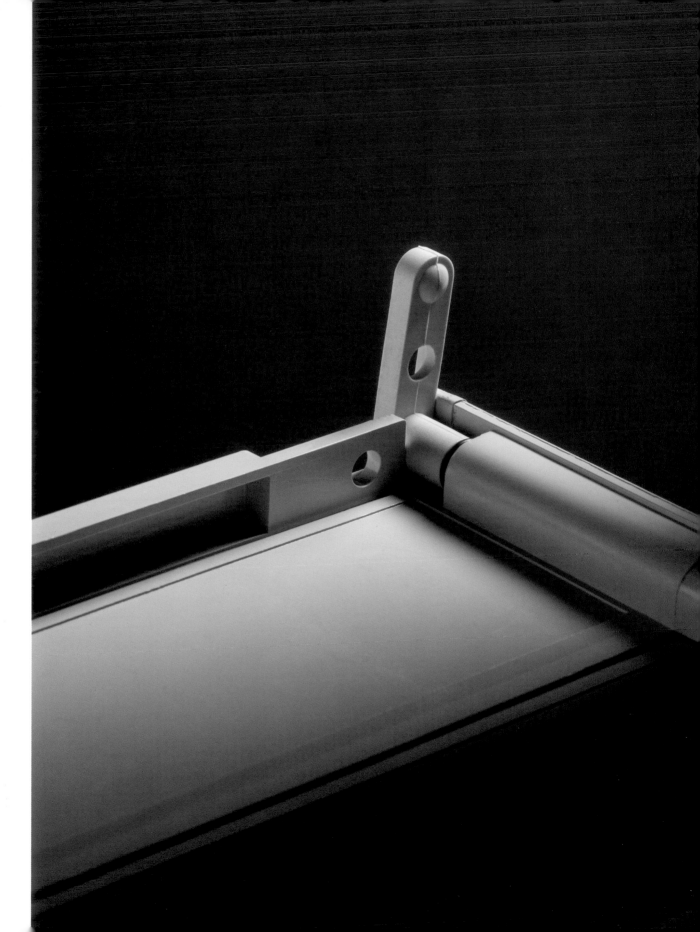

ORIGIN
United Kingdom

TECHNICAL DATA
ARM610 at 30 MHz, 32 MB RAM

AVAILABLE
April 1994

MANUFACTURER
Accrn Computers

Acorn's final line of computers was the RiscPC. With Windows all-pervasive and Intel releasing its newest range of microprocessors, the Pentium, Acorn responded by pushing more speed and better graphics in one of the most flexible home systems ever made. The RiscPC was a fascinating machine, built to support whatever its users wanted.

It was designed along the principle of 'slices'. BBC Micro case designer Allen Boothroyd returned to work with Acorn once again, dividing the RiscPC's case into layers that contained space for devices and expansion cards, which for some reason Acorn called 'podules'. The bottom slice held the machine's CPU and other fundamentals, and the second contained its CD-ROM and floppy drives, as well as space for two podules. Space for more devices could be added by fitting further slices on top; up to six slices could be added to the bottom one, making the RiscPC extraordinarily – and literally – expandable.

The RiscPC's extensibility didn't stop there. Up to 2 MB of dedicated video RAM could also be installed, raising the display's colour depth and resolution, but more significantly, the motherboard contained slots for 'host' and 'guest' microprocessors. The host was the machine's core processor, with the ARM610 being standard. But the guest slot could be fitted with a completely different processor, such as an Intel 486, allowing the RiscPC to support operating systems such as Windows 95. You could assign memory and a disk to it in RISC OS, and then the guest OS would run in a window.

Several new models and microprocessors were launched for the RiscPC over the next five years, but as a company Acorn found itself facing serious losses by 1998. A sequel, RiscPC 2, was cancelled, and Acorn laid off nearly half its staff as it refixed its focus on set-top boxes for digital TV, just like Amstrad before it. To emphasize the shift, it renamed itself Element 14 – a reference to silicon – but the company would never make another home computer.

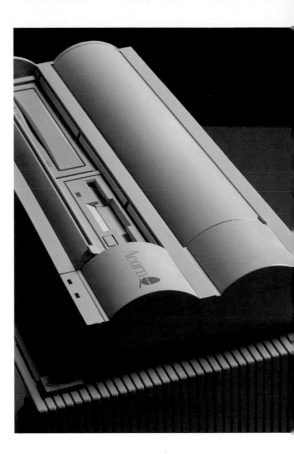

ACORN RISCPC 600

ORIGIN
United States

TECHNICAL DATA
PowerPC 750 G3 at 233 MHz, 32 MB
RAM

APPLE IMAC G3

AVAILABLE
August 1998

MANUFACTURER
Apple Computer

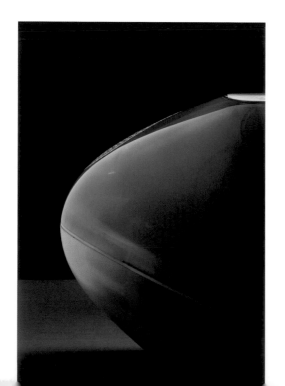

Apple had spent much of the 1990s in gentle decline, having failed to define a new product line as iconic as the Macintosh P.151. Its glumly named Quadra, Performa, and Centris lines were as beige as the boxes they attempted to compete with, and far more expensive because Apple aimed for high profit margins. Newton, an ARM-powered PDA, and W.A.L.T., a stylus-driven phone, could have defined whole new product categories, but Newton was crippled by a high price and issues with its handwriting recognition, and W.A.L.T. was never released.

And all the while, the PC continued to grow. While struggling to update its own operating system, OS 7, which launched in 1991, Apple attempted to sue Microsoft, claiming Windows' 'look and feel' was copied from Macintosh, but the case was thrown out because Apple had licensed its operating system to Microsoft in the mid-1980s. Apple's resurgence came in 1997 when Apple bought NeXT P.221, and with it, the leadership of Steve Jobs. Within a year, Apple was transformed, with a revitalized vision for what its computers should be, and the most advanced consumer operating system in the world.

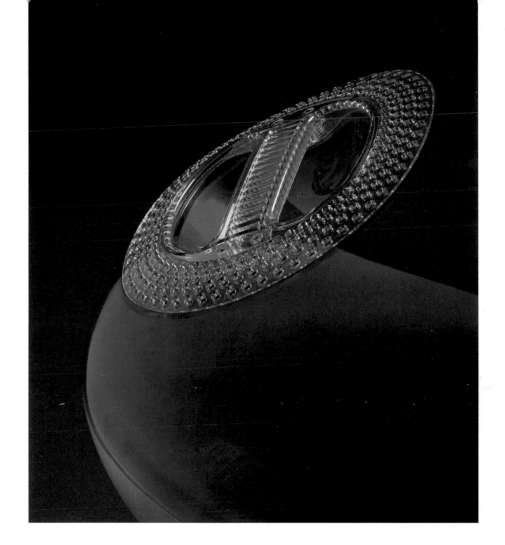

The iMac G3 was a symbol of all that had changed. After years of chasing the expensive end of the market, the iMac was designed for people. Its curved, semi-transparent case came in bright Bondi blue, making an appealing and tactile object out of a thing that was usually hidden under a desk or merely tolerated on top of one. Principally designed by Danny Coster and later developed by Jonathan Ive, it made a statement about the role of the computer: it should be part of the home. It was the first to ship with USB as standard – an interface that finally made it easy to plug any peripheral into a computer. And, equipped with ethernet and a modem, it also natively connected to the early Internet.

The iMac wasn't only a turning point for Apple; it also represented a watershed for the home microcomputer. Twenty-one years since the Apple II, PET, and TRS-80 kicked off the revolution, computers now played a role in every aspect of daily life. They were providers of entertainment, a place to create, a stage for communication, a source of information. The computer had evolved from a tinkerer's toy to a vital instrument of self-expression for all.

About the Author

Alex Wiltshire writes about videogames, design, and technology. He is author of several official books about Minecraft, including *Blockopedia* and *Mobestiary*; edited the book *Britsoft: An Oral History*; and contributed to *Design: The Whole Story*. He also writes for many publications, including *Edge*, *Disegno*, and *PC Gamer*. He lives in Bath, UK, with his wife and two children.

About the Collection

All machines featured are part of the collection held by The Centre for Computing History, Cambridge, UK

Published by arrangement with Thames & Hudson Ltd., London, by the MIT Press

Home Computers: 100 Icons that Defined a Digital Generation © 2020 Thames & Hudson Ltd, London
Text © 2020 Alex Wiltshire
Photography by John Short

Designed by Johanne Lian Olsen

ISBN 978-0-262-04401-1

Library of Congress Control Number: 2019948182

Printed in China by Midas Printing International Ltd

The MIT Press
Massachusetts Institute of Technology
Cambridge, Massachusetts 02142
http://mitpress.mit.edu